Joining AmeriCorps:

A Guide for Young Adults
Considering a Year of Service

Matthew Hudson-Flege
& Janna Pennington

www.joiningamericorps.com

Disclaimer: This book is solely the work of the authors. Information in this book does not necessarily reflect the opinions or official policies of AmeriCorps or related organizations.

Cover photo by Maura Carpinello, depicting (L-R): Jeanette Lesenko, Luke Greene, Kelsey McCarty, Tim Barr, and Andrea Rosado, Vincentian Volunteers of Cincinnati 2014-15.

For information, address: Trailside Publishing, LLC
www.trailsidepublishing.com
trailsidepublishing@gmail.com

ISBN: 979-8-9850937-0-4 (paperback)
ISBN: 979-8-9850937-3-5 (hardcover)
ISBN: 979-8-9850937-1-1 (ebook)

Library of Congress Control Number: 2021921124

Publisher's Cataloging-In-Publication Data
(Prepared by The Donohue Group, Inc.)

Names: Hudson-Flege, Matthew, author. | Pennington, Janna, author.
Title: Joining AmeriCorps : a guide for young adults considering a year of
    service / Matthew Hudson-Flege & Janna Pennington.
Description: [First edition]. | Greenville, SC : Trailside Publishing, 2021.
Identifiers: ISBN 9798985093704 (paperback) | ISBN 9798985093735
    (hardcover) | ISBN 9798985093711 (ebook)
Subjects: LCSH: AmeriCorps (U.S.)--Handbooks, manuals, etc. | Voluntarism-
    -United States--Handbooks, manuals, etc. | Volunteers--United States--
    Handbooks, manuals, etc.
Classification: LCC HN49.V64 H83 2021 (print) | LCC HN49.V64 (ebook) |
    DDC 361.370973--dc23

Matt's Dedication

To Katie, my parents, and the members of "Peter Green 4 Life," AmeriCorps NCCC Western Region Class IX. Thank you for supporting my AmeriCorps journey and helping me become who I am today.

Janna's Dedication

To the students and AmeriCorps members who have inspired me to dream big, listen well, and work hard for change. The world is better because of you!

Contents

Activity Pages

Note: All of the activities found in this book are also available online at www.joiningamericorps.com/activities. Use the password "AmeriCorpsActivities" to access the activities on the website.

Introduction

Are you interested in learning more about AmeriCorps? Welcome! We can't wait to tell you all about it! Whether you are reading this book because you're personally interested in joining AmeriCorps, or you are here to learn more for a student, your child, or another young adult you care about, this book is for you.

AmeriCorps is a nationwide network of programs engaging Americans in meaningful service to their country and their community. Often described as a domestic version of the Peace Corps, AmeriCorps members serve their fellow citizens in areas including education, environmental stewardship, and disaster preparedness and relief. AmeriCorps members work with nonprofit and public organizations, ranging from small neighborhood agencies such as your local foodbank, to nationwide networks like Habitat for Humanity or the American Red Cross.

AmeriCorps members are paid a living stipend to support them while they serve in AmeriCorps. After completing a term of service, they are eligible for money to support their education (either paying back student loans or paying for future education expenses). Currently, about 75,000 individuals serve in AmeriCorps each year. Some serve part-time or for a short period of time (i.e. summer), but for most individuals, AmeriCorps is a *year of service...* a full-time, roughly 10 to 12-month commitment that can be renewed for a second year. As you will learn in this book, exactly what service in AmeriCorps looks like depends a

1

great deal on the individual, the AmeriCorps program with which they serve, and their particular role within that program.

Because there are so many different AmeriCorps programs and ways to serve, it can be difficult to summarize in a concise definition. However, to sum it up briefly, here is how we define AmeriCorps:

Bringing out the best of America, AmeriCorps is a nationwide network of individuals and organizations who are getting things done for their communities through meaningful, paid service opportunities.

Why are you Reading this Book?

Are you a young adult interested in joining AmeriCorps? You are definitely in the right place. Besides giving you a chance to learn more about AmeriCorps, this book will help you figure out whether you should serve, how to find an AmeriCorps program that is the right fit for you, and how to make the most out of the experience during your AmeriCorps service and beyond.

Are you a not-so-young adult interested in joining AmeriCorps? Don't worry! There are lots of ways for adults of all ages to serve in AmeriCorps, whether full-time or part-time. While many aspects of this book focus on the unique transitions of a young adult serving in AmeriCorps full-time, we think you'll still find a lot of useful information here about how to serve in AmeriCorps.

Are you an educator or other person working with young adults who may want to serve in AmeriCorps? Thank you for being here! By reading this book, you will be well-equipped to answer questions about AmeriCorps and share information with young people who are interested in serving. We also hope that you will share this book with interested young adults so they can read it for themselves.

Are you the parent of a young person who wants to serve in AmeriCorps? We are thrilled that you are reading this book. AmeriCorps service can represent an incredible opportunity for your child. However, we're sure you have lots of questions, and we're confident that this book can answer many of them. We even have a section for you in the Appendix written by one of our parents!

About the Authors

Matthew Hudson-Flege, PhD, is a Research Assistant Professor at Clemson University, and the Program Director of a small AmeriCorps program, Furman College Advising Corps. Matt served in AmeriCorps after high school (more about that later) and also served in the Peace Corps in Jamaica after college. He has over a decade of experience working with AmeriCorps members in a variety of programs, and doing research on AmeriCorps members' motivation to serve.

Janna Pennington, M.Ed., is a personal and professional development consultant based in Greenville, SC. Before launching her consulting business, she spent 16 years teaching and advising college students and leading civic engagement programs at colleges and universities. She now works with AmeriCorps programs across the country to help members make the most of their experience and plan for their futures.

Together, the two of us have had countless conversations with young adults about what AmeriCorps is, whether people should serve, how to join, and how to make the most out of the experience.   We   have   done   our   best   to   translate   these conversations in this book.

About the Book

Now a quick note about what to expect in the chapters ahead. In the first three chapters of this book, you will learn about AmeriCorps, explore whether it's right for you, and find out how to search for programs that are a good match. Chapters Four and Five will help you prepare for life as an AmeriCorps member, get the most out of your experience, and plan for life after AmeriCorps. Finally, in the Appendices, we will share some alternatives to AmeriCorps for you to consider if you ultimately decide not to serve, and we also have a special note for parents of prospective AmeriCorps members.

Throughout this book, one of the things you'll hear repeatedly is that there are a wide variety of ways to serve in AmeriCorps, and a rich diversity in terms of who decides to serve. A question we often hear from young adults is if AmeriCorps service is the right fit for "someone like me." Rather than just take our word for it, we wanted to share the stories of four unique individuals who have served in AmeriCorps. As you'll see, they come from different walks of life, served in four very different AmeriCorps programs, and have since followed unique career and educational paths. We will briefly introduce them here, and you will learn more about their stories throughout the book.

AmeriCorps Member Profiles: Introductions

Ariel Cochrane-Brown

After growing up in North
Carolina and graduating from
UNC Chapel Hill with a degree
in Public Relations, Ariel was at
a crossroads. She didn't feel that
she was a "PR Girl" after all, but
she wasn't sure what she wanted
to do. After hearing about an
opportunity from a sorority

sister who had graduated before her, she decided to take a leap and
serve as a College Adviser through a program called College
Advising Corps. Together we will learn how Ariel's tentative leap
turned into two years of meaningful service and a rewarding career
in promoting college access for underrepresented students.

Alex Harvey

Alex grew up in Arkansas, and
after graduating from high
school he attended the
University of Arkansas to study
business. However, after a
couple of years, Alex felt that
college wasn't really for him, and
he was at a loss for what to do
next. After literally Googling

"What to do when you don't want to move back in with your

parents," Alex found out about AmeriCorps. He took a chance and moved to a new city, New Orleans, to serve with a housing and disaster relief organization called SBP. We will share Alex's story about how his year of service helped him discover his passion and kick start a successful career in property management and real estate.

Andrea Rosado

A self-described "Nuyorican," Andrea Rosado grew up in New York and attended the University of Notre Dame with the intention of going on to medical school. However, upon approaching graduation, Andrea felt a call to do more hands-on service, and knew she would need some additional time to apply to medical school. She ended up doing a year of service with a new, small program called Vincentian Volunteers of Cincinnati, working as a patient advocate in a charitable pharmacy. Follow along to hear about Andrea's experience with a year of intentional community and service, and how she ultimately went on to become Dr. Rosado!

Matthew Hudson-Flege

Yes, that's Matt, one of the authors! Matt grew up in Cincinnati, OH and graduated from high school in 2002. He had no interest in going right to college, and in the wake of the 9/11 terrorist attacks, was highly motivated to serve his country. However, with a newfound passion for community service that he developed through a mission trip, he didn't feel that military service was the right fit, so he wasn't sure what to do. Fortunately, his older sister told him about a program called AmeriCorps NCCC. He spent the next 10 months traveling around the country doing hands-on service with an incredible team of young  adults. In this book, we'll learn more about this experience, and how it started him off on a service oriented career that has taken him around the world.

***

Once again, we are thrilled that you have chosen to read this book! Whether you are interested in joining yourself, or are here to learn more for a student, child, or other person you care about, we appreciate your time and your desire to learn more about AmeriCorps. We hope that this book will answer many of the questions you have about AmeriCorps service and help you to find your best path forward. We believe that AmeriCorps service brings out the best of America, and we thank you for being a part of this movement!

***

Chapter One: What is AmeriCorps?

AmeriCorps members serving with City Year (Photo © City Year)

"AmeriCorps? What is that?" I (*Matt*) heard this question repeatedly when, as a high school senior, I told people my plans for the following year. To be honest, I got so tired of trying to answer this question that when asked by someone who wasn't a family member or close friend, I just lied and said that I was going to the University of Cincinnati. While the size, scope, and national awareness of AmeriCorps has certainly broadened in the last 20 years, it still isn't as widely known or understood as other national service options, namely the military or the Peace Corps (which is ironic given that there are currently about 10 times more AmeriCorps members than Peace Corps volunteers). In this chapter, we will examine the historical foundations, development, and current status of AmeriCorps. We will also outline some of the major AmeriCorps programs, and discuss what it means to be an AmeriCorps member. Our goal is for you to be able to answer the question: *what the heck is AmeriCorps?*

Historical Roots of AmeriCorps

In 1994, President Bill Clinton signed legislation creating the Corporation for National Service, and under its umbrella, AmeriCorps. Today, AmeriCorps members serve in diverse communities throughout the United States, working in areas ranging from disaster services, to education, to environmental stewardship. AmeriCorps can trace its roots to three prior domestic national service programs: the Civilian Conservation Corps, Volunteers in Service to America, and the National Civilian Community Corps.

The Civilian Conservation Corps (CCC), was a hallmark program of President Franklin Roosevelt's New Deal. By taking a walk or drive through almost any State or National Park in the country that is 75 years old or older, one is bound to see the legacy of this program firsthand. Immediately after taking office, President Roosevelt instituted a series of programs under the New Deal in order to combat the Great Depression, one of which was the CCC. The CCC served as both a government "relief" program aimed at providing employment and a modest income for young, unemployed men and their families, as well as a means to conserve the country's national and state forests. CCC members lived together in camps in forest settings, building roads and trails, constructing shelters, and planting trees in forests throughout the country.

In addition to the day-to-day work done by CCC members, the program also included citizenship and education components, with the goal of fostering active citizens who were better prepared to enter the workforce upon completion of their service. As Scott Leavitt of the U.S. Forest Service described, in the CCC "... the threatened resources of America's youth were sent to the rescue of the devastated and endangered resources of the forest. And it came to pass that in applying the remedies of regeneration to the land, the young men themselves have correspondingly and likewise benefited."[1] At the same time, by bringing Americans from diverse backgrounds to live and work together in the CCC camps, members gained a new appreciation for the country within which they lived and developed skills for living in community. As one former CCC enrollee described:

> *Ask a CCC veteran what he got out of the experience, and invariably his first response is that he learned to "get along with other people." But this doesn't mean an appreciation of ethnic or cultural diversity; it means something much simpler: this was often their first exposure to life beyond home, farm, [and] village. Thirty farm boys, city boys, mountain boys, all worked together. I was a farm kid. I didn't know how other people lived or what other people thought about the world. In the CCC we didn't have a choice, we had to work together and get to know each other.*[1]

---

[1] As cited in *The Politics and Civics of National Service*. Bass, M. Brookings Institution Press, 2013.

At its peak in 1935, the CCC enrolled more than 500,000 Americans per year, with more than 3 million total enrollees participating from 1933 to 1942. At the onset of World War II, however, the program was suspended due to the increasing demand for soldiers and workers in support of the war effort. Since the program was initially presented as a work relief program, in the booming postwar economy, proponents of the program were unable to make a sufficient argument to keep the program alive solely on the merits of civic education and community building. Nevertheless, in addition to the visible reminders still in existence in parks throughout the country, the ideological legacy of civilian national service initiated by the CCC lives on in the creation of AmeriCorps.

The second historical root of AmeriCorps is President Lyndon Johnson's Volunteers in Service to America (VISTA) program. Created in 1964 under the Economic Opportunity Act, more commonly known as the "War on Poverty," VISTA engaged approximately 5,000 young Americans per year in service to impoverished communities until it was incorporated under the AmeriCorps umbrella in the early 1990s. In many ways, VISTA resembled a domestic version of the Peace Corps. Projects were proposed by local and state governments and typically involved teaching or capacity building in neighborhood organizations. In addition to this direct service work, however, VISTA members often became involved in community organizing and efforts to promote democratic participation among the poor. This aspect of VISTA, however, was highly politicized, with the Johnson and Carter administrations promoting higher levels of community organizing within VISTA, and the Nixon, Reagan, and Bush administrations promoting a focus on direct service. Unlike the CCC, VISTA never grew to become a large, widely known program. However, it survived several decades and presidential administrations, helping to establish a more permanent role for civilian national service. The program still continues today under the AmeriCorps umbrella.

The third important predecessor of AmeriCorps is the National Civilian Community Corps (NCCC). In 1992, with the Cold War at an end and anticipated military downsizing on the horizon, President George H.W. Bush created NCCC, intending to provide a strong alternative to military service by combining the best elements of civilian and military service. Teams of 18 to 26-year-olds were assembled in bases throughout the country to work on projects in the areas of disaster relief, environmental protection, education, and unmet human needs. Drawing on the traditions of the military, NCCC members wore uniforms, participated in physical training, and were often led by retired members of the military (former Drill Instructors leading long-haired hippies in PT... they really should have made a reality show about this!). Drawing on the history of the CCC, members received a modest living and educational stipend, and focused on domestic, civilian service. Unlike the CCC or the military, however, NCCC was a small program, engaging only 1,200 members per year. Nonetheless, NCCC helped create a bridge between the distant predecessor of the CCC and the modern AmeriCorps programs of today, and as with VISTA, would be rolled up under the umbrella of AmeriCorps in 1994.

Development of AmeriCorps Today

In 1994, shortly after taking office, President Bill Clinton created the Corporation for National and Community Service (CNCS). This new entity expanded and incorporated the fledgling NCCC program within the AmeriCorps umbrella, together with AmeriCorps VISTA and a variety of AmeriCorps State and National programs. While funding for AmeriCorps as a whole would be threatened in congressional budgets multiple times over the next 15 years, the program received bipartisan support and a sense of ownership from Presidents Clinton, Bush, and Obama, as well as congressional leaders such as the late Sen. John McCain. In 2020, CNCS underwent a rebranding, where the entire agency simply became known as AmeriCorps. Currently, there are more than 75,000 active AmeriCorps members serving at any given time.

AmeriCorps programs fall into four major categories: AmeriCorps VISTA, AmeriCorps NCCC, AmeriCorps State and National, and AmeriCorps Seniors. AmeriCorps VISTA continues its original tradition of engaging individual volunteers in year-long capacity building projects at community-based nonprofit organizations aiming to alleviate poverty. Likewise, AmeriCorps NCCC also continues in its original vein, engaging 18-26 year olds in a team-based, 10-month program providing service in the areas of disaster relief, environmental stewardship, education, and unmet human needs. The largest of the three AmeriCorps program categories, AmeriCorps State and National, involves hundreds of local, state, and national organizations. Nonprofits, faith- and community-based organizations, tribal nations, and public agencies apply for grants from AmeriCorps State and

National to engage AmeriCorps members in paid service programs. State and National programs range from small initiatives engaging a handful of members at one local organization, such as Vincentian Volunteers of Cincinnati, to large, national programs such as City Year, which places hundreds of members in 29 high-need school districts throughout the country. The final category, AmeriCorps Seniors, provides a variety of ways for Americans ages 55+ to serve their communities. Since this book is focused on young adults interested in AmeriCorps, we won't discuss AmeriCorps Seniors further. However, if you are interested in learning more about this awesome program, check out https://americorps.gov/seniors.

While there are many part-time AmeriCorps positions available, AmeriCorps members most commonly serve full-time for approximately 10-12 months, receive a modest living stipend and other benefits, and an education award (currently $6,345) upon completion of their year of service.

Major AmeriCorps Programs

One of the great things about AmeriCorps, but also one of the things that makes it a bit confusing, is the broad diversity of AmeriCorps programs and ways that members can serve. AmeriCorps members serve in all 50 US states (and multiple territories), and work in settings ranging from a school classroom, to a home construction site, to a cubicle at a nonprofit, to a trail on the side of a mountain. In this section, we will provide more details about AmeriCorps NCCC, AmeriCorps VISTA, AmeriCorps State and National in general, and a few major AmeriCorps State and National programs (City Year, College

Advising Corps, Habitat for Humanity, and American Conservation Experience).

AmeriCorps NCCC
https://americorps.gov/nccc

 @AmeriCorpsNCCC

 @AmeriCorpsNCCC

 @americorpsnccc

AmeriCorps NCCC is a unique, team-based program that provides a variety of hands-on service projects. AmeriCorps NCCC members must be between the ages of 18-26, and serve between 10-12 months depending on their specific program option. AmeriCorps NCCC teams consist of 10-12 members, and work on a series of short-term projects throughout their term of service (typically a minimum of four projects in different cities and states around the country). There are two program options in AmeriCorps NCCC. "Traditional Corps" engages NCCC teams in projects with community organizations focused in the areas of energy conservation, infrastructure improvement, disaster relief, and community development. "FEMA Corps" teams support the Federal Emergency Management Agency (FEMA) with a variety of projects related to disaster preparedness and recovery.

To serve in AmeriCorps NCCC, individuals apply directly to the program, and if accepted, receive an assignment to one of four regional campuses (Pacific Region- Sacramento, CA; North-Central Region- Vinton, IA; Southwest Region- Aurora, CO; Southern Region- Vicksburg, MS). Within the program, there are two possible roles: NCCC Member and NCCC Team Leader. NCCC members learn a variety of new skills through a three-week training known as the Corps Member Institute. Similarly, Team Leaders are assigned to a regional campus, complete training through the Team Leader Institute, and are then assigned to a team of AmeriCorps members who they will guide and support throughout the year. At the end of training, teams are assigned to diverse projects over the course of their term of service in states and territories throughout their region. Teams live and work together throughout their term of service. Altogether, these experiences provide AmeriCorps NCCC members with unparalleled opportunities for personal and professional growth. At the same time, the unique demands of the program require members to be flexible, adaptable, and open to new experiences!

AmeriCorps VISTA
https://americorps.gov/vista

 @AmeriCorpsVISTA

 @AmeriCorpsVISTA

Building on the tradition established in 1965, AmeriCorps Vista members help to fight poverty by supporting the capacity of nonprofit organizations and public agencies throughout the United States. While VISTA members' individual job descriptions will vary, common activities include grant writing and fundraising, volunteer recruitment, and research. VISTA members serve in an office setting, and work for a single organization for a one-year term of service. Placements with AmeriCorps VISTA can include local to national nonprofits, public agencies, or colleges and universities. As with AmeriCorps NCCC, there are two types of positions available: VISTA Member and VISTA Leader, with VISTA Leaders supporting and guiding other VISTA Members at their organizations.

To serve in AmeriCorps VISTA, individuals apply directly for specific positions at organizations. These positions can be found both through the AmeriCorps website, as well as job postings at local nonprofit organizations and public agencies who host VISTA members. VISTA members must be at least 18 years of age, and there is no upper age limit to serve. One unique aspect of AmeriCorps VISTA is that members receive Non-Competitive Eligibility (NCE), which gives them an edge when applying for jobs with the federal government in the future. Additionally, AmeriCorps VISTA places an emphasis on professional development training. The experience with capacity building work, professional development opportunities, and Non-Competitive Eligibility make AmeriCorps VISTA an excellent option for individuals who are interested in a career in the nonprofit or public sector.

AmeriCorps State and National
https://americorps.gov/serve/fit-finder/americorps-state-national

AmeriCorps State and National provides thousands of opportunities for AmeriCorps members to serve in communities throughout the United States. AmeriCorps positions are hosted by nonprofit organizations, ranging from small organizations serving a single community, to statewide agencies, to nation-wide initiatives. Positions vary greatly from organization to organization, but are all focused on serving communities in the areas of education, environmental stewardship, economic opportunity, disaster response, community well-being, or serving veterans and military family members. While it would be impossible to describe every AmeriCorps State and National program in a single book, we have included descriptions of four nation-wide programs in order to give you an idea of the types of positions available through AmeriCorps State and National. To find AmeriCorps State and National positions near you (or in an area you would like to live and work), see Chapter Three in this book for tips on how to organize your search.

City Year
www.cityyear.org

 @CityYear

 @cityyear

 @cityyear

City Year was founded in 1988 as an opportunity to engage young adults in a demanding year of full-time community service, and is today one of the most prominent AmeriCorps State and National programs. Wearing their trademark City Year jackets, members serve in 29 cities across the country. City Year members work in diverse teams as student success coaches in schools, building relationships with students, leading afterschool programs and activities to support an environment where students can thrive, and providing one-on-one and small group tutoring and mentoring for students. City Year members participate in training prior to beginning work in their assigned school, and engage in additional training and leadership development opportunities throughout the year.

To serve in City Year, individuals must be between the ages of 18 and 25, and have a high school diploma or GED. Individuals apply for the program directly through City Year's website, and can specify either a city or region where they wish to serve or indicate that they are willing to serve wherever they are needed most. With a rich history and a broad network of partners and alumni, serving in City Year can open doors to a wide variety of educational or professional opportunities. Approximately half of City Year alumni continue to work in the education field after completing their service.

American Conservation Experience (ACE)

https://www.usaconservation.org/

 @usaconservation

 @usaconservation

 @americanconservationexperience

Founded in 2004, American Conservation Experience is a national leader in engaging volunteers in environmental restoration projects through a service learning model across the United States. ACE has AmeriCorps positions located throughout the country through two main programs: Conservation Crew and Emerging Professionals in Conservation (EPIC). In Conservation Crew, AmeriCorps members ages 18-35 work in professionally supervised teams as they explore future outdoor careers, learn practical field skills, and develop confidence as emerging leaders in the field of conservation by doing hands-on work such as trail-building, ecological restoration, wildlife monitoring and non-native species removal. The ACE/EPIC program provides AmeriCorps members individual placements and fellowships, giving recent college graduates focused, hands-on opportunities to work alongside and under the guidance of agency mentors as they apply their knowledge of resource management on their path to becoming the next generation of resource and land managers.

Working alongside staff from the National Park Service, U.S. Forest Service, Bureau of Land Management, U.S. Fish and Wildlife Service, and many other public land agencies, AmeriCorps members serving with ACE gain invaluable career perspectives and mentorship in a variety of areas. Individuals interested in serving with ACE can find and apply for positions directly through ACE's website. Positions are typically full-time, and range from three to nine months. There are also opportunities to move up in the program as Assistant Leaders or program staff members. The focus on environmental stewardship work, and accompanying learning opportunities offered throughout the term of service, make ACE a great program for individuals interested in a career related to environmental stewardship. However, it also provides an excellent opportunity for personal growth and self-exploration for individuals with a wide variety of long-term interests.

Habitat for Humanity AmeriCorps

www.habitat.org/volunteer/long-term-opportunities/americorps

 @HFHAmeriCorps

 facebook.com/groups/HabitatAmeriCorps/

Founded in 1976, Habitat for Humanity strives to build homes, communities, and hope throughout the United States (and in more than 70 countries around the world). As a volunteer-driven organization, local Habitat organizations throughout the country engage AmeriCorps members in a variety of roles to support their efforts to build and maintain affordable housing. While positions vary, common AmeriCorps State and National positions available with Habitat include Construction Crew Leader, Volunteer Services Coordinator, Community Outreach Coordinator, and Homeowner Services Coordinator. In addition to these positions, several local Habitat organizations also host AmeriCorps VISTA positions related to capacity-building efforts.

AmeriCorps positions with Habitat are most commonly full-time, roughly one-year positions, although some part-time positions are also available. Individuals interested in serving with Habitat AmeriCorps can search the website for positions by city and state, and can also find AmeriCorps position postings on the website of a local Habitat organization in their area. Depending on the focus of the AmeriCorps position chosen, serving as an AmeriCorps member with Habitat can open doors for a broad range of career opportunities.

College Advising Corps
www.advisingcorps.org

 @AdvisingCorps

 @advisingcorps

 @advisingcorps

College Advising Corps (CAC) is the nation's largest nonprofit service organization focused on opening higher education's doors to all, especially those from low-income, first-generation, and underrepresented communities. In partnership with 34 colleges and universities throughout the country, CAC matches AmeriCorps members from their corps of recent college graduates with under-resourced high schools to help students find and pursue their best higher education path. In addition to one-on-one advising, College Advisers also organize events that help to build a college-going culture in their school. CAC near-peer advisers are embedded into low-income, underserved high schools for a one- to two-year service engagement as full-time College Advisers that serve all students.

To serve in College Advising Corps, individuals must have recently earned a bachelor's degree, in any major. Individuals apply directly to a university-based program, and information about each chapter can be found on College Advising Corps' website. College Advisers participate in summer training to prepare for the year ahead, as well as additional training and professional development opportunities throughout the school year. While its focus on educational advising makes College Advising Corps a great fit for individuals interested in working in school counseling or higher education, the skills and experiences gained can translate to a broad range of graduate school or career opportunities.

What it Means to be an AmeriCorps Member

As you have seen above, there are a wide variety of ways to serve in AmeriCorps, so the day to day experience of AmeriCorps members will vary greatly. That being said, there are some things that all AmeriCorps members have in common:

You are a member (not a volunteer). Individuals serving in AmeriCorps are referred to as "members" and not "volunteers" for two reasons. First, unlike a traditional "volunteer" at a community organization, AmeriCorps members are compensated for their time through a living stipend and an Education Award. Second, as an AmeriCorps member, you *belong* to a large (and growing!) network of individuals who have served their country in AmeriCorps and are committed to staying involved in their communities long after their year of service comes to an end.

You receive a living stipend. AmeriCorps members are paid through what is known as a "living stipend." In some AmeriCorps programs, such as College Advising Corps, this stipend will closely resemble the salary of an entry-level professional position, and you will be expected to cover typical bills (rent, transportation, food, cell phone, etc.) with this stipend. In other programs, such as AmeriCorps NCCC, the living stipend will be much more modest, but some of your essentials such as housing, transportation, and/or food may be covered by the program. Be sure to research the specifics of the living stipend when applying for a program!

24

You receive health insurance and other benefits. All full-time AmeriCorps members receive health insurance while serving, and childcare benefits may also be available. Additionally, AmeriCorps members are eligible for loan forbearance on federally-guaranteed loans while they serve. Again, be sure to research the specific benefits offered by particular AmeriCorps programs when applying.

You receive an Education Award. At the conclusion of a successful term of service, AmeriCorps members receive a Segal AmeriCorps Education Award. As of this writing, the Education Award amount for a full-time term of service is $6,345 (the exact amount changes year-to-year, and is tied to the amount of a Federal Pell Grant). Funds from the Education Award can be used to either pay for future educational expenses (tuition, books/supplies, room and board, etc.) or to pay back student loans. To learn more about the Education Award and how to use it, see Chapter Five of this book or visit https://americorps.gov/members-volunteers/segal-americorps-education-award.

You serve for a specific amount of time. AmeriCorps members commit to serving for a specific term of service, most commonly 10-12 months depending on the program (although summer and part-time positions are also available). AmeriCorps members may serve additional terms in either their current AmeriCorps program or another program. However, AmeriCorps members are limited to receiving two full Segal AmeriCorps Education Awards, which effectively limits most individuals to serving two years in AmeriCorps. The specific timeframe of AmeriCorps programs makes it an ideal option for young adults to gain skills and experience during a transition period before, during, or after college, or before launching their careers.

You wear a uniform. AmeriCorps members represent the program by wearing an AmeriCorps uniform. In some programs, such as City Year, this may be a full uniform including distinctive shirts, jackets, etc. In other programs, you may be wearing business casual attire, but have the AmeriCorps logo on your nametag. In any case, you are representing the broader AmeriCorps community to your organization and the community you serve.

You "Get Things Done" for America. Whether working with students, building a trail in a park, helping a nonprofit organization write a grant, or serving meals in a hurricane shelter, AmeriCorps members pledge to "get things done" for their fellow Americans. This means not only doing your best during your year of service, but also applying the skills and experiences you gain as an AmeriCorps member to make positive contributions to your community long after your year of service comes to an end.

You grow. Whatever AmeriCorps program you choose, you will have an opportunity to build relationships with new people, experience a new community, or take a deeper dive into your own community. Serving in AmeriCorps provides an unparalleled opportunity for you to learn new professional skills and grow as a person.

AmeriCorps Member Profiles: How they Served

You've just read a lot about the history of AmeriCorps, what it looks like today, and different ways to serve. But what does this look like in real life? Let's take a look at the ways that Ariel, Alex,

Andrea, and Matt served in AmeriCorps. In the coming chapters, we will learn more about why they served, where they are now, and what advice they have for you.

Ariel Cochrane-Brown: College Advising Corps

After graduating from UNC Chapel Hill with a Journalism degree (with concentration in Public Relations), Ariel became a College Adviser with College Advising Corps, which you just read about earlier in this chapter. Ariel served students at two high schools in North Carolina, helping them and their families along the journey to post-secondary education. A "normal" day for Ariel consisted of meeting one-on-one with students, calling up parents or college admissions reps, planning and running events at the school, and everything in between! For Ariel, her year of service was an opportunity to step into adulthood very quickly. She had to learn how to interact with students as a "near peer" to whom they could relate, while at the same time presenting herself as an authoritative professional. She also had to learn skills like time management and budgeting, working a demanding job, and living on a modest living stipend.

In spite of these challenges, she had an incredibly supportive site supervisor at her school, who she remains close with as a mentor today. She also has fond memories of working with individual students, in particular a young woman who was about to age out of foster care and didn't have a clear plan after high school graduation. Ariel recalled crying tears of joy after learning this young woman had been accepted to college with a scholarship and housing package after it seemed like no options would be available to her.

Alex Harvey: SBP

When life as a college student wasn't working out for Alex and he needed a new direction, Alex became an AmeriCorps member with SBP (https://sbpusa.org/). Founded in Louisiana in response to Hurricane Katrina, SBP works with homeowners to prepare for and rebuild after natural disasters. SBP hosts AmeriCorps State and National members in several states and territories across the country. As an AmeriCorps member, Alex relocated to New Orleans to serve as a Client Services Coordinator.

In this role, Alex helped to facilitate assistance for families through three programs: home rehabilitation for families whose homes had been damaged in natural disasters; rental property management for low-income families; and facilitating mortgages for low-income families to purchase their own homes. During his time with SBP, Alex got to learn the ins and outs of the property management and real estate business, and learned how to work with people from different backgrounds. In fact, Alex still exchanges messages with an individual he helped move into a home! He also got to experience life in a brand new city, and make valuable professional connections.

Andrea Rosado: Vincentian Volunteers of Cincinnati

After graduating pre-med from the University of Notre Dame, Andrea joined Vincentian Volunteers of Cincinnati, which is a small, faith-based year of service program hosted by St. Vincent de Paul, a nonprofit organization in Cincinnati, OH (VVC; https://www.svdpcincinnati.org/vvc) For a year, Andrea lived in community and worked in the West End of Cincinnati with four other AmeriCorps members (see them all on the cover photo!).

During her time with VVC, Andrea served as a Patient Advocate in St. Vincent de Paul's Charitable Pharmacy. In this role, she met one-on-one with patients to help them enroll in the Charitable Pharmacy program so they could receive their medication at no cost, and assisted them with other services through referrals. In addition to this day-to-day work, Andrea played a leadership role in ensuring that materials throughout the organization were available in both English and Spanish, and also established a partnership with another local organization, the Good Sam Free Clinic, to help put translation services in place for patients.

During this year of service, Andrea gained valuable experiences in building relationships with patients and others, learning how to advocate for her patients, and living and working with people from different walks of life. It also provided her with a year to prepare for and apply to medical school.

Matthew Hudson-Flege: AmeriCorps NCCC

After graduating from high school in Cincinnati, OH, Matt moved across the country to serve as a member of AmeriCorps NCCC based in Sacramento, CA. As you read earlier in this chapter, AmeriCorps NCCC provides a variety of hands-on service opportunities for 18-26 year olds. For 10 months, he served on a team of 11 individuals, working on different projects across the western United States. His team's projects included leading volunteers at the San Francisco Food Bank; working with young students in an elementary school in Sacramento; building trails near Big Sur, California; planting native trees in Salt Lake City, Utah; and running summer programs for youth in the small old-west town of Virginia City, Nevada. While doing these projects, his team lived together, with lodgings ranging from a small apartment in San Francisco, to a cabin in the woods, to a church basement. As you can imagine, Matt got to try his hand at many different types of work, including manual labor, volunteer management, and tutoring. This allowed him to not only gain new skills, but also identify types of work that he really enjoyed (as well as figure out what types of work he did not enjoy!). But in addition to the work experience, serving in AmeriCorps NCCC allowed him to build friendships with a group of incredible people from all over the country. It was also a crash-course in "adulting," as he went from being a high school kid living at home, to a member of a team who was expected to pull his weight not only at work, but also in the kitchen cooking and cleaning for the team!

***

Now back to the question I (*Matt*) faced when I was in your shoes… *what the heck is AmeriCorps?* As you have seen, given the rich diversity of AmeriCorps programs, there is no simple, universal answer to that question. At the end of the day, it will depend on you and how you choose to serve. But whichever path you take, serving in AmeriCorps means that you will get things done for your country and community, you will gain skills and experiences that can kick start your education or career, and you will have an unforgettable experience!

Chapter Two: Should I Join AmeriCorps?

AmeriCorps members serving with American Conservation Experience
(Photo © American Conservation Experience)

Working with college students and prospective AmeriCorps members, we are often approached by students (or their parents/teachers) with the question, "Should I join AmeriCorps?" While we almost always ultimately encourage the student to apply, the reasons why they should join AmeriCorps and the type of AmeriCorps program that would make the most sense for them vary greatly based on the individual. In this chapter, we will discuss the diverse groups of individuals who serve in AmeriCorps and some myths about serving in AmeriCorps. With this information, we hope that you will be able to affirmatively answer the question of whether you should join AmeriCorps.

Idealists, Wanderers, Gappers, and Servants, Oh My!

As you learned in the first chapter, there are more than 75,000 individuals serving in AmeriCorps at any given time, and there are thousands of different ways to serve. So when thinking about who serves in AmeriCorps, why they serve, and how service impacts them, it is important to keep this rich diversity in mind. Through analyzing data from surveys completed by thousands of AmeriCorps members, personally interviewing AmeriCorps alumni, and our own experience serving in AmeriCorps and leading AmeriCorps programs, we have identified four broad "profiles" of young adults who serve in AmeriCorps: Young Idealists, Wanderers, Gappers, and Public Servants. These profiles are certainly not exhaustive, and are not meant to put individuals into a box. However, it is our hope that by presenting these profiles, you may be able to further explore the reasons why you are interested in serving with AmeriCorps and know that there are others out there who have similar interests as you.

Young Idealists: *Recent High School Grads out to Save the World*
Young Idealists are recent high school grads with a high level of motivation to serve and make an impact on their community. They join AmeriCorps because it provides an opportunity to do meaningful, hands-on work. Of course, they probably have long-term goals and plans in terms of education and career, but serving in AmeriCorps allows them to start doing the work here and now, not in the distant future. Young Idealists bring unrivaled energy and enthusiasm to the table, which serves them well doing the difficult work that a year of service with

32

AmeriCorps often entails. At the same time, they may also be somewhat naive about the world and have unrealistic expectations about the impact they will make as an AmeriCorps member. But by pushing through the hard lessons that they will learn about the world and themselves, they can get things done during their year of service. They can also put themselves in position for successful, service-oriented careers in the future.

Wanderers: *Young Adults Searching for Purpose and Direction*
Wanderers are a bit older than Young Idealists. They have graduated from high school, and may have a couple years of college or work experience under their belt. However, the college or career path they have been on just hasn't felt right, and they are looking for something more. They like the idea of doing meaningful work during a year of service, but most of all, AmeriCorps seems like a great opportunity to learn about themselves and find a sense of purpose and direction. Wanderers bring creativity and a sense of humility to the table, which is an important trait in doing community development work. They also tend to be a bit more timid, and may also get frustrated when the sense of direction they are looking for doesn't jump out clearly during their service. However, by reflecting on their accomplishments throughout their year of service and being open to the many learning opportunities presented through their work with AmeriCorps, they can be effective members. They can also leave with a stronger sense of what they are looking for in life and in their careers.

Gappers: *Recent College Grads Seeking a Meaningful Gap Year*

Gappers are recent college grads who look to AmeriCorps as an opportunity to do meaningful work after graduation while planning for the next step in their career. Some Gappers, like the Wanderers, may be feeling a bit lost as they approach graduation and are seeking a sense of direction. Other Gappers may have a clear idea of the next step in their career (professional or graduate school, an entry level position in their career field, etc.), but they want to take an opportunity to do meaningful work and have an interesting life experience before buckling down in their career. In either case, as college graduates, Gappers bring experience and competence to the table as AmeriCorps members. Because they may not have been as active in community service or similar experiences as other AmeriCorps members, however, the sometimes harsh realities they will face as AmeriCorps members may have a tough impact on them. But by keeping an open mind and learning from their peers, Gappers can make a positive impact and experience tremendous personal growth during a year of service with AmeriCorps, setting them off on the right foot as they begin their professional careers.

Public Servants: *Recent College Grads Launching a Career in the Nonprofit/Public Sector*

Public Servants are recent college grads, with a high level of service motivation, who join AmeriCorps as a way to kick start a career in the nonprofit, public, or helping professions. For some, AmeriCorps might represent an opportunity to gain a year or two of valuable experience and get a foot in the door at a nonprofit organization, which can be a challenge for recent college grads with limited work experience. For others, they may have plans for graduate or professional school, and look to AmeriCorps as a way to bolster their résumés while taking the time to explore graduate school options and apply. As college graduates with often significant volunteer, work, or internship experience, Public Servants bring competence and leadership to the table, allowing them to be highly effective AmeriCorps members. At the same time, like Young Idealists, they may grow frustrated if they feel their ideas aren't heard within their organization or program. But by recognizing their AmeriCorps experience as an opportunity for continued learning and growth, they can not only serve as productive AmeriCorps members in the present, but also launch a meaningful long-term, service-oriented career.

AmeriCorps Member Profiles: Why Did They Join?

Let's check back in with our four new AmeriCorps alumni friends to learn why they joined AmeriCorps.

Alex Harvey: The Wanderer

When Alex realized, as a student at the University of Arkansas, that college just wasn't a good fit for him at the time, he was at a loss for what to do. He was interested in a career in real estate, and he was also interested in trying out life in a big city. However, he really didn't know how to make the leap to get there from where he was at the time. When he Googled, "what to do when I don't want to move back in with my parents," he found AmeriCorps, so he began looking further.

After searching for positions in a variety of platforms, he found out about SBP. The organization's housing-related focus seemed like it might give Alex some experience and connections in the world of property management and real estate. There were also positions available in New Orleans, which seemed like an exciting place to live for a year. When he was offered a position after applying, he decided to take a risk, move to a new city, and give AmeriCorps a shot!

Andrea Rosado: The Public Servant
As Andrea approached her senior year of college, she knew that ultimately she was on a path to medical school and a career as a doctor. However, she also knew that she didn't want to jump right from college to medical school. First and foremost, she wanted an opportunity to be involved in meaningful, person-to-person service that went deeper than the volunteer experiences she had in college. She also wanted an opportunity to better understand issues of poverty and justice, which she hoped she would one day be in a position to address as a doctor. Finally, she was looking for an opportunity to grow personally. Spending a year living in community with a group of people she had never met and taking on a challenging role as an AmeriCorps member certainly seemed like it would fit the bill!

Additionally, Andrea had some very concrete, practical reasons for joining. First, she felt that she would need some additional time to submit applications and interview for medical schools, and serving in AmeriCorps would give her the time to do that while also bolstering her résumé. Secondly, for personal reasons, Andrea was interested in living in Cincinnati, OH (sorry to call you out here, Andrea, but by "personal reasons" we mean "boyfriend"). Vincentian Volunteers of Cincinnati presented a way to check all of these boxes.

Ariel Cochrane-Brown: The Gapper

Ariel's service as an AmeriCorps member with College Advising Corps started off with a chance request. While she was a junior in college, she got an email from an older sorority sister who was currently working in a high school, and needed volunteers to help with a "college application day" event. She signed up, not so much out of a strong desire to serve, but more-so because of the "big sister – little sister" sorority dynamic. However, she had a great time volunteering at the event, and began to learn from her big sister what College Advising Corps was all about.

Fast forward to a year later, and Ariel was approaching graduation with the realization that she had zero interest in a career in public relations after all. When she got an email from career services about applying to serve with College Advising Corps, she remembered her sorority sister, and thought to herself, "maybe this is something I could do." She applied, was accepted, and was happy to report to her mom that she had a job lined up before she graduated! Little did she know that this "two year" stint with College Advising Corps would set her on a completely different career path.

Matthew Hudson-Flege: The Young Idealist

As a senior in high school, Matt sat in a classroom and watched the twin towers fall in the terrorist attacks on 9/11. Like many of his classmates, Matt was caught up in a wave of patriotism and a desire to serve his country. However, at the same time, he had also recently developed a passion for volunteering and community service that came about from participating in some mission trips through his high school. Joining the military didn't quite seem like the right fit, but he wasn't sure how else he could serve his country full-time.

It was at this time that his older sister, who was doing an internship for AmeriCorps headquarters as a college student, sent him a brochure for AmeriCorps NCCC. He was intrigued by the opportunity to be of service, to experience different places and different types of work, and to meet people from all over the country. It seemed like the perfect opportunity for a motivated young high school grad who wanted to do hands-on service. While a lot of people (his parents, included) were confused about what AmeriCorps was and wondered why he wasn't going to college, he decided to take the risk. After getting accepted to the program he boarded a plane for California!

***

Whether you can relate to the Young Idealists, Wanderers, Gappers, or Public Servants (or maybe some combination of them), it is important to reflect on where you are in your life and why you want to serve. What are the things in your life that you have been passionate about, or have brought you joy? What are things you have struggled with? What made you consider a year of service with AmeriCorps in the first place? What skills and experiences can you bring to the table as an AmeriCorps member? What do you hope to get out of the experience? Only by thoroughly evaluating these questions can you decide if a year of service with AmeriCorps is right for you, and if so, what type of AmeriCorps service represents your best path forward.

AmeriCorps Myths

Also important in helping you decide whether you should join AmeriCorps is dispelling some common myths about AmeriCorps service. Again, as we have said and will continue to say throughout this book, your experience with AmeriCorps will vary greatly depending upon the program in which you serve. However, these are some pretty common myths about AmeriCorps:

Myth 1: *You will waste a year that you could have been in school or working.* The concern that a year in AmeriCorps could be better spent in school or working is a common refrain from individuals who are thinking about AmeriCorps but can't quite make the leap, and also from many parents of prospective AmeriCorps members. For high school graduates, there is the concern that if they don't go right to college, they may never go (Matt certainly heard this from his dad before he joined AmeriCorps NCCC!). For recent college grads planning on graduate school, there is often a concern that during a year of AmeriCorps, "I might get out of 'school mode,' and it will be really hard to go back." Finally, there is the concern that by taking a year to serve in AmeriCorps instead of directly entering the workforce in your career field, you will fall behind.

First, for the high school graduate (or the college student thinking of taking a break), it is true that, statistically speaking, people who don't go right to college are less likely to eventually earn a degree. However, it is important to note that taking a gap year to do AmeriCorps is *very* different than just "not going to college" or "dropping out." If approached correctly, a year in AmeriCorps can be spent learning about yourself and your interests, and figuring out an educational path that is right for you. It is also an opportunity to earn an Education Award and bolster your résumé, which may increase your education and scholarship options. Consider this: less than half of Americans who currently earn a bachelor's degree do so in four years. For some, a year in AmeriCorps can replace a year of trying to "figure out your major" while paying college tuition. So if a college degree is your ultimate goal, taking some time out to serve in AmeriCorps can be time well spent.

For college graduates who have graduate or professional school aspirations, a concern we often hear about serving in AmeriCorps is that if they take a year or two away from college, it will be harder for them to get back into "student mode" in graduate school. There are three counters to this argument. First, it's important to point out that graduate school is very different from undergrad; it's not simply a 5th and 6th year of college. You are often expected to work as a graduate assistant, and the courses are typically more independently-driven and project-based. In our experience, the skills needed to succeed in graduate school often more closely resemble the skills learned through professional experience, rather than simply being a good "student." A year or two of progressive responsibilities in AmeriCorps can certainly translate to the work you will do as a graduate student. Second, graduate school is expensive. By serving in AmeriCorps, you will earn an Education Award, and many graduate schools offer a matching program or other special financial aid for AmeriCorps alumni. Furthermore, if you are applying for a graduate assistantship, in many cases having a year or two of AmeriCorps experience will make you much more competitive than if you are applying right out of undergrad. Finally, with the wide variety of graduate school programs offered today, it is important to note that attending graduate school (whether full- or part-time) will almost certainly be an option for you in the future. However, as you get older and take on increasing responsibilities (family, career, mortgage, etc.) the chance to serve as a full-time AmeriCorps member becomes more challenging. In particular, if you are thinking about a residential, hands-on program such as AmeriCorps NCCC or a Conservation Corps, the year after college graduation may be your best opportunity.

Finally, for those who have a good sense of the type of work they want to do, but are interested in taking a year out to serve in AmeriCorps, there is a concern that they will "fall behind" a year in your career compared to if you had simply gone ahead and gotten a "real job." Again, let us present you with three counter arguments to this notion. First, in a survey of over two thousand AmeriCorps members, as well as about two thousand individuals who were interested in AmeriCorps but ultimately did not serve, AmeriCorps members reported learning significantly more professional skills than their peers who did not serve in AmeriCorps. Organizations engaging young adults as AmeriCorps members usually have significant professional development opportunities built into the program, and AmeriCorps members are often given more leadership opportunities than they would be in a typical entry-level job. This can mean that while you may have waited a year or two to get that "real job," when you do get there, you will often have a leg up in terms of skills and experience. Second, it is also important to consider that by serving in AmeriCorps, you may be qualified for a broader range of "real jobs" than you would be applying for jobs straight out of school. Many jobs, even at the entry level, require a year or two of professional experience, particularly in the nonprofit and public sectors. AmeriCorps service provides an excellent opportunity to gain this experience and bolster your résumé. Finally, even if you were to literally fall behind one year in promotions and raises by serving in AmeriCorps, in the long run, how important is this? If you are currently in your late teens or early twenties, consider that you most likely have a 40+ year career ahead of you. There will be ups and downs to your career that you can't even imagine right now. It is alright to take time now to do something that you think will be meaningful for you.

Myth 2: *You can join AmeriCorps if you're not yet ready to get a real job.*
One sentiment we often hear, particularly from college seniors approaching graduation, is that they are interested in joining AmeriCorps because they aren't yet ready to commit to a "real job." However, as you are learning, the work you do as an AmeriCorps member will be very real, and very demanding. Indeed, in many cases, AmeriCorps members are often given significantly more responsibility, autonomy, and leadership opportunities during their year of service than they would in a typical entry-level job. As an AmeriCorps member, you will be asked to put in long hours, and often do work that can be mentally and emotionally draining. If you are dedicated to your AmeriCorps service, you will almost certainly have put in as much or more time and effort as you would have in any other job.

On the flip side (and where the sentiment of this myth may come from), doing a year or two of service with AmeriCorps does tend to give you more flexibility than taking a typical job, particularly right after college. As a time-limited program, you know going in that you are only committing to a specific amount of time (typically around a year) to whatever program you join, which can certainly be appealing if you aren't yet sure of what you want your career to look like. One or two years serving in AmeriCorps is a strong résumé booster for future employers or graduate school. In contrast, taking a "normal" job with an organization and then leaving after a year may be a red flag to prospective employers. At the same time, most AmeriCorps programs offer support for you as you try to identify your long-term interests and next steps in your career, whereas a typical employer may be most interested in keeping you where you are. To be sure, AmeriCorps does present an alternative to the long-term commitment that may come along with a "real job." Just understand that it is not an alternative to putting in the work!

Myth 3: *You can't get by on an AmeriCorps living allowance.*
No, you will not get rich during your AmeriCorps service. However, you will not starve either! As discussed earlier in this book, the living stipend offered by different programs can vary greatly, and this is an important thing for you to consider when selecting a program. However, all full-time AmeriCorps programs offer health insurance benefits (among others), and when applying to host AmeriCorps members, organizations must demonstrate that their members can get by in the local community based on the living stipend and other supports (housing,

transportation, etc.) that may be provided. All this being said, getting by on an AmeriCorps living stipend can require careful planning and some sacrifices (see Chapter Four for some tips). While you will certainly not get rich during a year of service with AmeriCorps, you'll also want to take into account the value of the Segal AmeriCorps Education Award, and additional scholarship or assistantship opportunities that can come from serving in AmeriCorps. If you are willing to carefully budget and prioritize (skills that will serve you well for life!), you can get by as an AmeriCorps member.

Myth 4: *You will save the world!*
This one is for you Young Idealists and Public Servants out there. Yes, you will absolutely have an opportunity to make a positive impact as an AmeriCorps member. You could be helping a child learn to read, working with a family to rebuild their home after a natural disaster, or building a trail that will allow people to experience the beauty of nature. You *will* get things done during your year of service. However, there will also be days when you are spinning your wheels and feeling like you aren't accomplishing anything. Whether it is the interpersonal difficulties that arise from working with individuals and families, the limited resources that come with working in a nonprofit organization, or the frustrating red-tape that comes in the public sector, we promise you there will be times when you're frustrated and you question whether you're making an impact. And for many AmeriCorps members, the "work" they accomplish during their year of service may never quite live up to their expectations.

The key to dealing with this is keeping an open mind about what success looks like, and maintaining the long view. Yes, a year or two in AmeriCorps is a significant amount of time, and it is important to feel a sense of accomplishment from all of the hard work that you put in. At the same time, as a young adult, it is also important to keep in mind the long life and career that you have ahead of you. The experiences you gain, and the often difficult lessons you learn during your time in AmeriCorps, will influence you for the rest of your life. Know that the work you're doing now can help to make you a more well-rounded person, a more effective professional, and a more committed family and community member in the future. No, you will not save the world during your time in AmeriCorps. But you will make an impact, however modest, and you will set yourself up for a lifetime of creating positive change in the world around you.

Myth 5: *You will "find yourself."*
Now a myth for the Wanderers and Gappers. Don't get us wrong, a year of service with AmeriCorps is going to provide a ton of opportunities for self-discovery and growth. However, without being very intentional about your experience, your sense of purpose and direction isn't going to suddenly come to you in a magical revelation. During your AmeriCorps experience, you will need to work hard to reflect on the experiences you are having, the people you are meeting, and the work you are doing in order to draw out what these experiences can tell you about who you are as a person, and what you want to do with your life. You will need to be open to learning from others, and seek out mentors who can share their experiences with you. Also recognize that these

mentors may not only be leaders at your organization, but may be your fellow AmeriCorps members, folks in your community, and the individuals you serve. Finally, you will need to be comfortable knowing that the things you learn about yourself and the plans you develop for your future will change over time, and that is ok!

If you are comfortable with some uncertainty and putting in the work, a year of service with AmeriCorps can indeed provide you with unparalleled opportunities to learn about yourself and explore different paths for your future. You will encounter new people, places, and experiences, and do so in a supportive environment with people who are genuinely interested in your growth and development. So while it is not realistic to expect to suddenly "find yourself," serving in AmeriCorps can certainly help to point you in the right direction and set you off on a lifelong path of self-discovery.

Myth 6: *You will be lonely.*
For some AmeriCorps members, who find opportunities to serve in the communities where they grew up or currently live, this may not be much of a concern. However, for those who will be relocating to serve, often in unfamiliar areas, this may be a fear. You will be leaving behind your friends and family, your classmates, and the familiar comforts of your home or your college community. And while this is a valid, natural fear any time you are moving to a new place or starting a new phase in life, the reality is that by serving in AmeriCorps, you will be surrounding yourself with an incredible group of new individuals with whom you can form relationships. Whether it's your fellow AmeriCorps members, other coworkers at the organization where you serve, or

the neighbors in your new community, you will have a chance to develop rich friendships with people from different walks of life. Indeed, the friendships you form during a year of service with AmeriCorps may be some of the strongest of your life.

On the other hand, if you do choose to serve in AmeriCorps in your hometown (or the community were you currently live), it is important to take the time to form relationships with your new peers. It can be easy to want to head home after a tough day and surround yourself with the comfort of your existing friends and family. However, if you lean too heavily in this direction, you may miss out on some incredible new friendships. Additionally, if you think of yourself as an ambassador for your community to your fellow AmeriCorps members who may be from out of town, you can not only form meaningful new relationships, but also grow a new appreciation for your community by seeing things through a new lens.

All this being said, the work you are doing will be difficult, and as an AmeriCorps member, there may be times where your role is unique and you do feel isolated and alone. This is a natural feeling in any new job, and it's ok to feel this way from time to time. But by being open to forming supportive relationships with those around you, you will most certainly not be lonely during your year of service with AmeriCorps.

***

Now you have heard a bit more about different types of people who join AmeriCorps and why they join, and you have considered some different myths and realities about what a year of service with AmeriCorps may be like for you. Are you ready to answer the question: *Should I join AmeriCorps?* If you're still on the fence, here are a few more suggestions as you discern whether or not AmeriCorps is for you:

- **Talk to a mentor:** Think of a teacher, school counselor or adviser, supervisor, or other person in your life who knows you well and whom you respect. Tell them about what you're considering, and see what questions they have for you to consider or what input they have.

- **Talk to your family and friends:** Tell your family and friends about AmeriCorps and your interest in joining. As people who know you well, they may have some great insights for you.

- **Talk to an AmeriCorps Member/Alum:** If you are still in school, ask around to see if anyone can put you in touch with a graduate of your school who is a current or former AmeriCorps member. Do any of your family members or friends know someone who has served? If you are interested in a specific program, could they put you in touch with one of their members? Hearing someone's personal experience can be incredibly valuable. However, keep in mind that everyone's experience is unique!

- **Continue Reading:** In the next chapters of this book, we will talk about strategies for finding an AmeriCorps program that is the best fit for you, how to get the most out of a year of service with AmeriCorps, and how to prepare for life after AmeriCorps. Or, if you ultimately decide AmeriCorps is not the best fit for you, we also discuss other options for you to consider in the Appendix.

Talking to others and doing your research can certainly help as you make your decision. However, as an adult, it is ultimately your decision to make! You know yourself best. Weigh your options and consider the advice of others, but trust your instincts and do what feels right to you. Ultimately, if you do decide to join AmeriCorps, and commit to putting in the effort to prepare and make the most out of it, we are confident that you will be setting yourself up for an unforgettable experience of making an impact and growing as a person.

Chapter Three: How do I Join AmeriCorps?

AmeriCorps members in College Advising Corps working with students.
(Photo © College Advising Corps)

One of my (*Matt's*) ultimate guilty pleasures here in South Carolina is a fast-food restaurant called Cook Out. If you've never lived in the Southeast, you probably haven't had the privilege of eating at Cook Out, so let me break it down for you. At Cook Out, when you order a combo tray, you have a choice of 16 different main items ranging from a quesadilla, to barbecue, to a burger. Then you choose two of their ten different side items, or double up on one. Finally, you choose a beverage, and here the choice gets easy… you want a milkshake! However, depending on the time of year, you have 41+ flavors to choose from such as chocolate chip mint, banana fudge, or just plain old vanilla. All told, there are literally thousands of possible combinations for how you could order your meal! So while saying to myself, "today is a Cook Out kind of day" is the first step in getting lunch, there are still some pretty important decisions to make before I can enjoy that milkshake.

Deciding that you are going to join AmeriCorps is kind of like deciding on Cook Out for lunch. With a number of diverse programs and positions all across the United States, you have literally thousands of ways to serve in AmeriCorps. Figuring out how to join and exactly which path to take can be almost as daunting as ordering the right milkshake (alright, maybe slightly more daunting!). In this chapter, our goal is to help you go from saying "I want a milk shake," to decisively stating "I would like a Chocolate Chip Cheesecake milk shake, please." And hey, just in case they are out of that particular flavor, we'll help you be ready with a couple of exciting back-up options.

In order to narrow down the thousands of ways to serve in AmeriCorps to the path that you will actually take, there are three questions to consider. First, how do I find AmeriCorps positions? Second, how do I figure out what AmeriCorps position is right for me? Finally, how do I prepare a successful application? Let's dive into each of these questions.

Finding AmeriCorps Positions

When looking for AmeriCorps positions, there are a few different approaches you can take. Depending on your interests and what you're open to, you will probably want to try a combination of these approaches. The main ways we recommend to find AmeriCorps positions include:

1. Searching the AmeriCorps website
2. Searching the Service Year Alliance website
3. Searching the website of your State Service Commission (or the state(s) where you'd like to serve)
4. Searching specific organization websites
5. Searching a general job-posting website such as Indeed.com

Below, we will describe each of these approaches in more detail. We will include some specific website links, but please keep in mind these things change so you may need to do some Googling!

Searching the AmeriCorps Website

https://americorps.gov/serve/fit-finder

On the AmeriCorps website, you will find a description and link to the pages of each of the major AmeriCorps programs that we described in Chapter One, including AmeriCorps NCCC, AmeriCorps VISTA, and AmeriCorps State and National (as well as AmeriCorps Seniors programs for individuals 55+). Depending on which type of program(s) you're interested in, your destination from here will vary:

If you are interested in AmeriCorps NCCC, clicking the link to the specific NCCC website (https://americorps.gov/nccc) will take you to a comprehensive page with a breakdown of what AmeriCorps NCCC is all about, ways to serve, benefits, and how to apply. With AmeriCorps NCCC, you will fill out one single application to be considered for the program. On the application, you can indicate what region(s) you're interested in, whether you're interested in the traditional AmeriCorps NCCC or FEMA Corps, and whether you're interested in serving as a member or a Team Leader. AmeriCorps NCCC has three start dates each year (Summer- July/August; Fall- October; Winter- February) so you will want to be sure to pay attention to when the application deadline is for each cycle. Finally, if you have questions about the application process for AmeriCorps NCCC, they have even developed a comprehensive guide for you at https://americorps.gov/serve/fit-finder/americorps-nccc/join/guide.

If you are interested in AmeriCorps VISTA or AmeriCorps State and National, clicking on the link to the specific VISTA website (https://americorps.gov/vista) or the State and National Website (https://americorps.gov/serve/fit-finder/americorps-state-national) will again take you to a comprehensive page describing what each program entails, ways to serve, benefits, and how to apply. However, with AmeriCorps VISTA and AmeriCorps State and National, you don't apply directly to the program (like with NCCC), but instead find and apply for specific positions open at organizations throughout the country. From the AmeriCorps VISTA or State and National websites, if you click on the link to "begin your search" you will be taken to the AmeriCorps Advanced Listing Search (which you can also access by visiting www.my.americorps.gov and clicking "Search Listings"). From here, you can do a "Quick Search" where you just select one or more of the following: AmeriCorps program type, State, and/or

Program Name. More likely, however, you will want to do an "Advanced Search."

With an Advanced Search, you will be able to refine your search based on several criteria, including:

- Program type (State and National or VISTA)
- Service term (full-time, part-time, or summer)
- Education requirement (high school diploma/GED, associate's, bachelor's, etc.)
- State(s) where you want to serve
- Metro area(s) where you want to serve
- Service areas (environment, education, health, etc.)
- Any additional language(s) you speak
- Special skills you would like to use while you serve

After you enter your various search terms, you will get a list of specific positions that are available. By clicking the link to a particular position, you'll find out more details about that position and a link to apply.

If you're following along, or have already checked out the AmeriCorps website's search page, you might be wondering why you need to search for positions anywhere other than the AmeriCorps website. Well, the major limitation of the AmeriCorps website is that *not every available AmeriCorps position is posted on the AmeriCorps website.* We won't get too far into the weeds here, but because AmeriCorps positions are decentralized among many different organizations across the country (both large and small) and because of issues related to the timing of receiving AmeriCorps funds, not every organization can or will post their open positions on the AmeriCorps website. Bottom line: if you are interested in AmeriCorps NCCC, the

AmeriCorps website is your best and only way to apply. If you are interested in AmeriCorps VISTA and/or AmeriCorps State and National, the AmeriCorps website is a good place to start and will present you with some options, but you will want to do additional research to find all the opportunities that are out there.

Service Year Alliance
https://serviceyear.org

Service Year Alliance is a national organization whose mission is to make a full-time, paid year of service a common expectation and opportunity for young Americans. Their bold goal is to see one million Americans engaged in service each year! As part of this mission, Service Year Alliance has built ServiceYear.org, a platform which contains rich resources for current AmeriCorps members, host organizations, alumni, and importantly for you, individuals seeking out a service year opportunity.

ServiceYear.org has a search page where you can look for full-time service year opportunities, a large majority of which are AmeriCorps positions, and also provides suggested matches to apply for based on your preferences. You can search for positions based on geographic location (city or state), focus area (disaster relief, homelessness, etc.), and when the position begins (currently hiring, 6 to 9 months, etc.). There are also several more advanced search fields including, but not limited to location type (rural, urban, etc.), benefits, and activity type (hands on, office, etc.). The platform is very user friendly, and the variety of search fields can really help you find positions that will meet your needs and goals.

However, as with the AmeriCorps website, it is important to note that *not every available AmeriCorps position is posted on this website.* Service Year Alliance is still a relatively young organization, but continues to grow in prominence and popularity with organizations who host AmeriCorps members, so more positions are listed each year. Like the AmeriCorps website, this is a good place for you to do a nationwide search for AmeriCorps opportunities, but probably won't be the only place you should look. And remember, once you do join AmeriCorps, ServiceYear.org will have some great resources for you!

State Service Commissions

Many organizations that host AmeriCorps members are funded and organized through what are known as State Service Commissions. State Service Commissions provide funding for AmeriCorps positions, and provide training and other support for AmeriCorps organizations and their members. All 50 states, as well as many territories (Puerto Rico, Washington D.C., etc.), have a Service Commission. To find the website for the Service Commission in the state where you live (or in the state(s) where you would like to serve), you can do a Google search for the name of your state + "State Service Commission (i.e. "South Carolina State Service Commission"), or you can view a list of all State Service Commissions at https://americorps.gov/contact/state-service-commissions.

A State Service Commission's website will typically have two important resources to help you find an AmeriCorps position. First, they may have a list of current AmeriCorps positions available in the state or a search page where you can look for open positions. However, an important thing to keep in mind is that depending upon the time of year you are doing your research, AmeriCorps programs may not be actively recruiting. For example, if you are doing your research in November, but the organization you're interested in starts new AmeriCorps members every August (which is quite common), they probably won't have positions listed as available until sometime in the spring.

For this reason, the other helpful resource that you can find on a State Service Commission's website is a list of all the organizations in the state that receive AmeriCorps funding. Depending on the state, this may be a simple list, or again it might be a more extensive search page where you can look for organizations based on focus area, geographic location, etc. Typically, you will find the name of each organization, a brief description of the work they do and possibly what types of AmeriCorps positions they have, and a link to each individual organization's website. By looking through a listing of AmeriCorps organizations in your state, rather than just what positions are currently open, you will get a much more comprehensive picture of what kinds of opportunities are out there. Build a list of organizations you are interested in, and then proceed to our next step.

Specific Organization Websites

Once you know of a specific organization you are interested in that hosts AmeriCorps members (whether through searching a State Service Commission website, word of mouth, or somewhere else), you will want to look at their specific website to learn more about AmeriCorps opportunities that are available. Again, if they don't have any positions listed right now, don't get discouraged, as AmeriCorps recruiting is often seasonal. Rather, do some research on their website to learn more about what types of AmeriCorps positions are typically offered, when they are usually recruiting, benefits, and how to apply.

For some organizations, all of this information will be spelled out very clearly on their website. For others, it may be a bit more limited. Regardless, a great next step when you have found an organization you are interested in is to reach out directly to a staff member to find out more. Try to find out from the website who is specifically in charge of the AmeriCorps program (or for larger organizations, AmeriCorps recruiting) and give them a call or send them an email. Introduce yourself, express your interest in becoming an AmeriCorps member with their program, and ask questions you have about the program or the application process. Doing so will not only help you find out more information about what positions may be available and how/when to apply, but will also let the program know that you are a serious candidate.

General Job Posting Websites

One final place to look for AmeriCorps positions is on general job posting websites such as www.indeed.com. This is a good option if you have a specific geographic area in which you want to serve. On Indeed's website, typing the word "AmeriCorps" into the "What" search field, and a city, state, or county where you're interested in serving in the "Where" search field will generate a list of current job postings that have the word "AmeriCorps" in them. When most organizations post AmeriCorps positions, they will either have the word "AmeriCorps" somewhere in the job title or in the job description, so doing a search like this on Indeed.com will generate a pretty comprehensive list of current opportunities.

However, as discussed earlier, AmeriCorps recruiting is often seasonal, so what you find on a job search website today is different from what you will find next month. One strategy to address this on Indeed is to set up a job alert email based on your "AmeriCorps" keyword and location search. The other solution, as discussed earlier, is to research specific organizations that host AmeriCorps members so you'll know when positions typically become available.

***

While we wish there was one simple, single place to look for AmeriCorps opportunities, that unfortunately is not the case. However, by going through the resources described above, with a bit of patience and persistence, you will quickly find yourself with a long list of AmeriCorps service opportunities. The good news is you will have a lot of options. The bad news is we're back to the Cook Out milkshake situation, where it can be easy to become paralyzed by FOBO (fear of a better option). Don't dismay, the following pages will help you find your best fit!

Finding your Fit

With all of the AmeriCorps possibilities out there, how can you possibly choose the "right" one? First, some general life advice: sometimes there isn't one "right" answer. When choosing an

AmeriCorps program (or any job, career, or educational path for that matter) know that there are probably several options that could make sense for you in different ways. Regardless of what you choose, it will be up to you to make the most out of wherever you end up. All that being said, this is a major life decision, so you'll want to think through the important parts of a potential AmeriCorps opportunity, and make sure that they align with your needs and goals. When evaluating an AmeriCorps position, there are three key areas that you'll want to consider: the job; the logistics; and the "intangibles." Below, we will describe each of these areas, and then present you with a worksheet you can use to evaluate AmeriCorps positions you're considering.

For *the job*, you'll want to consider the nature of the work you'll be doing as an AmeriCorps member, and what your day-in and day-out work routine will entail. What is the main focus area(s) of the position (education, homelessness, environmental stewardship, etc.) and how passionate are you about this area? What are the key responsibilities that an AmeriCorps member has in this position, and how do they fit with your interests? What is the type of work (hands-on tasks, personal interaction, administrative, etc.), and how does this fit with what you like to do? What is the actual workplace setting where you will spend your time (office, classroom, in the field, etc.), and can you picture yourself spending your days there?

Moving beyond the work you would be doing as an AmeriCorps member in a particular position, there are some key logistics to consider. First, where is the position located, and how do you feel about this location? What is the living allowance provided to AmeriCorps members, and can you feasibly get by on this amount (See Chapter Four for tips on budgeting)? What other benefits might be provided to AmeriCorps members (healthcare, professional development opportunities, housing, etc.)? Finally, what housing options would be available if you took this position? This could entail housing provided by the organization, living at home if the position is in your area, or renting a place (possibly with fellow AmeriCorps members or other roommates). Give some thought to how you feel about these potential housing scenarios, and also think about what your daily commute might look like.

Finally, you'll want to think through some of the "intangibles" of the position. These are hard to quantify, but let's try to describe them! First, as most AmeriCorps positions are hosted by a nonprofit organization, you will want to consider the organization's mission. All nonprofit organizations have a mission statement which guides their work, and some organizations will also lay out a more detailed vision statement and values. How does the organization's mission statement align with your values? Second, as much as possible, you'll want to try to get a feel for the culture of the organization as a whole, and their AmeriCorps program specifically. How does this culture fit with your personality? For this, it may be helpful to talk to AmeriCorps alumni who have served at the organization. Finally, what are the group dynamics for this position? Are you serving as part of a team of fellow AmeriCorps members or other staff at the organization, or will you be working more independently? Again, how does this fit with your personal style?

After considering these specific aspects of a position (the job, the logistics, and the intangibles), you can step back and ask yourself some broader reflection questions to evaluate if the position is a fit for you. What do you love about the position? What are you nervous about? How does it fit with your skills and personality? How might you grow in the position? Finally, knowing that AmeriCorps service is a short-term step in your longer career, how does the position fit your long-term goals?

At the end of this chapter on page 67, we have provided a worksheet that you can use to evaluate different AmeriCorps positions (or visit www.joiningamericorps.com/activities to download a copy). As you go through this activity, keep in mind that different aspects of a position will carry different weight for you, so there is no numeric "score" that you can use to make a decision of what is right for you. Ideally, you will find at least a couple of AmeriCorps positions where you feel you can do satisfying work in the short-term, grow as an individual, and prepare for the next step in your career. While no position is perfect, we're confident that there are some great AmeriCorps service opportunities out there for you!

Preparing a Successful Application

Alright, you have scoured the AmeriCorps website, local job postings, and the websites of local organizations to find several open AmeriCorps positions. You've used the worksheet at the end of this chapter to narrow the list down to a few options that you are really excited about. Now what? Time to apply!

Not to sound like a broken record here, but how hard it is to successfully apply for an AmeriCorps position varies greatly depending on the organization and the actual position. Some AmeriCorps programs, such as Teach for America, are extremely competitive, with tons of qualified applicants who must go through a multi-stage application and interview process. Other programs, particularly smaller organizations in more rural areas, struggle every year to find enough members to fill their positions. Regardless, you will want to put your best foot forward when applying and interviewing for any AmeriCorps position. Having hired many AmeriCorps members over the years, here are our tips:

Reach out Personally: As mentioned earlier in this chapter, it can be a good idea to reach out personally to a staff member at an AmeriCorps program to introduce yourself and ask questions. For a large program, like City Year, this may involve filling out an online form to speak with a recruiter. But for a small organization, this probably means calling up the staff person who manages the AmeriCorps program (usually with a job title like "program director" or something similar). In either case, reaching out before you apply can help to a) answer any questions you may have about the program and application process and b) make you a "known entity" to the program. When someone is reviewing multiple job applications to try to narrow a long list of candidates to a short-list of people to interview, anyone who has reached out beforehand to ask thoughtful questions is naturally going to rise to the top of the list.

Prepare your Professional Profile: Hopefully in Chapter Two, we dispelled the myth that serving in AmeriCorps isn't a "real job." As such, you will want to approach applying for an AmeriCorps position with the same level of seriousness and preparation as applying for any other professional position. What does that mean? Well, here are just a few steps: prepare a crisp, professional résumé and cover letter that you can tailor to different applications; have a professional-sounding email address (as close to firstname.lastname@gmail.com as possible) that isn't tied to a school; clean up your social media presence and create a LinkedIn page. If you are a college student (or recent alumni), be sure to take advantage of your school's career services center for help. If you are in high school, ask your guidance counselor and/or career facilitator for help!

Articulate your "Why": I'll never forget when, as a high school senior doing a phone interview for AmeriCorps NCCC, I (*Matt*) was asked, "Why do you want to join AmeriCorps?" I was so excited about the program and knew it was perfect for me, but I hadn't really thought through how I could communicate this to someone else. Needless to say, I stumbled through my answer and talked a lot longer than I needed to. While this didn't end up costing me in the end, you will want to be prepared to clearly and concisely explain why serving in AmeriCorps in general, and the specific program/position you're applying for in particular, is a good fit for you. You'll need to do this both in writing when you apply, and verbally during an interview. Clearly and confidently explaining how you can make a positive contribution as an AmeriCorps member, and how the position fits with your long-term goals, will go a long way in your application or interview.

Follow Instructions: Like just about everything else we've discussed so far, the actual application process itself will vary greatly based on the AmeriCorps program. For some programs, you'll need to fill out a lengthy online form and submit accompanying materials, similar to a college application. For other programs, the instructions will simply be to email a copy of your résumé and cover letter to the program director. In either case, you will want to carefully follow all instructions. For an online application, make sure you complete all fields, attach all requested documents, and meet all deadlines. For an application that asks you to send in a résumé and cover letter, make sure you include any specific information they have asked for, and be sure to tailor your cover letter to this specific application. Going back to our first tip, if you have a question about the application, ask!

Be Yourself: AmeriCorps staff know that oftentimes, this might be the first full-time, professional position you've applied for. They are not expecting you to walk into an interview with the same amount of confidence and polish as a mid-career professional. Rather, they are looking for someone who is honest, willing to learn, and who has a passion for the type of service they will do as an AmeriCorps member. If you have to try to present a different version of yourself in an interview, trust us, it will show, and it is probably a sign that this position isn't the right fit for you!

***

While it can be daunting to track down what AmeriCorps opportunities are out there, figure out which ones are the right fit for you, and make your way through a variety of applications and interviews, we hope that the tips presented in this chapter will make it more manageable. Try to keep an open mind and stay positive throughout the process. If you do this, we're confident that you can join AmeriCorps!

Activity 1: AmeriCorps Position Evaluation Worksheet

Organization Name: _____

Position Name: _____

Dates: *App. Deadline:* _____ *Start:* _____ *End:* _____

Instructions: Use this worksheet to help evaluate whether a position is a good fit for you. In the table below, jot a couple of notes next to each aspect of the position and check a box for the emoji showing how you feel about it. Then, answer the reflection questions below.

	🙁	😐	🙂
The Job			
Focus Area(s):			
Key Responsibilities:			
Type of work:			
Workplace Setting:			
Logistics			
Location:			
Living Allowance:			
Other benefits:			
Housing options:			
Intangibles			
Organization Mission:			
Organizational Culture:			
Group Dynamics:			

What do I love about this position?

What am I nervous about?

How does this position fit my skills & personality?

How will I grow in this position?

How does this position fit my long-term goals?

Chapter Four: Making the Most of Your Service Year

An AmeriCorps member serving with Habitat for Humanity
(Photo © Habitat for Humanity of Greenville County)

Now that you have decided to join AmeriCorps, it's time to start thinking about how to make the most of your service year. In this chapter, we will explore some of the opportunities and challenges that you may encounter and provide tools to help you prepare for your AmeriCorps experience. Some of these tools will help you tackle things like budgeting and time management, while others will help you prepare mentally and emotionally.

One way that you can begin to prepare mentally is to make sure you have a *growth mindset* going into your service year. People who have a growth mindset are interested in learning new things and developing themselves both personally and professionally. They are not afraid to challenge themselves and they see obstacles as opportunities for growth rather than reasons to quit. When things don't go as planned, they adapt and look for ways to make the most of their circumstances. Having a growth mindset is the first step towards making the most of your AmeriCorps experience!

Opportunities as an AmeriCorps Member

Joining AmeriCorps is a great way to serve others and make an impact in your local community, but there's more to the AmeriCorps experience than community service. During your year of service, you will have opportunities to grow personally and professionally and develop skills that you will use in your future career. It is important that you begin your year of service not only ready to serve, but ready to learn as well. Here are a few of the opportunities you'll enjoy as an AmeriCorps member:

Career Development
While some AmeriCorps members choose to serve in areas that will provide them with professional experience in their chosen career fields, others begin their service unclear about their future career plans. Whether or not you know what you want to do with your life, AmeriCorps will provide excellent opportunities for you

to gain experience, build your résumé, and explore various career options. The knowledge and skills you gain during your service year will make you more marketable to future employers, and the experience of serving with a community organization may help you decide what type of career may be a good fit for you. Try to keep an open mind, viewing each assigned task as a chance to learn and prepare for your future career (more about this in Chapter Five).

Networking

"Networking" is a fancy word for building professional relationships and making connections in your career field. When you join AmeriCorps, you become part of local and national networks that can provide resources and support during and after your year of service. Take advantage of the opportunity to connect with other individuals who share your passion for improving communities. You never know when these connections may lead to a friendship, partnership, or future job opportunity! Make the most of these networks by initiating conversation with people who are doing work that interests or inspires you. Sure, it may be uncomfortable to contact someone you've never met, but there can be many benefits to doing so.

Financial Benefits

As you know, AmeriCorps members enjoy many financial benefits, including a monthly living stipend and the Segal AmeriCorps Education Award, which can be used for student loan repayment or future education expenses. Other financial benefits include student loan deferment and interest forbearance, as well as health insurance. You can read more about these benefits in Chapter Two.

Personal and Professional Development

Perhaps one of the greatest benefits of AmeriCorps service is the personal and professional development opportunities that the experience affords. As an AmeriCorps member, you will have the chance to learn about yourself and others and develop new skills that you can use in your future career.

However, in order to take advantage of these opportunities you'll need to begin your year of service with an open mind and a willingness to learn. Remember the growth mindset that we mentioned at the beginning of the chapter? If you are feeling anxious about how you will perform in your new job, remember that no one expects you to show up on the first day with everything figured out. Even if you work hard, you will still make mistakes, and that is ok! Rather than getting discouraged, ask yourself what you can do differently next time. The goal is not for you to perform perfectly, but for you to finish your AmeriCorps service with more skills and awareness than you had when you began.

It may be helpful for you to consider the areas where you would like to grow before you begin your service year. Would you like to improve your time management? Do your public speaking skills need some work? Are you interested in learning what it takes to lead a non-profit organization? Setting goals now will help to ensure that you make the most of your AmeriCorps experience. There will be more about that later, but in the meantime, here are some areas where you might like to grow and develop:

- **Self-awareness:** How well do you know yourself? Self-awareness is understanding your personality, thoughts, feelings, and behaviors.

- **Leadership:** Do you have what it takes to lead others towards a goal? Leadership may include some of the other areas listed here, including communication, problem-solving, and self-awareness.

- **Problem-solving:** Are you equipped to deal with the challenges that come your way? Problem-solving skills are important in all areas of life.

- **Oral and written communication:** Can you express yourself in a professional manner and convey ideas through written and spoken communication? Sometimes people think this is an area where they are either talented or not, but communication is a skill in which we can all improve!

- **Time management:** Juggling multiple responsibilities can be challenging. How well can you organize and plan your time?

- **Interview skills:** Are you prepared to answer questions and confidently describe your qualifications in a job interview?

- **Teamwork:** How well do you work with others? Teamwork requires listening and learning from others' perspectives when working toward a common goal.

- **Budgeting:** Financial management is important for everyone and learning to create a budget is an essential skill for young adults.

- **Event planning:** Large-scale events require a lot of coordination and logistics management. Are you interested in developing your abilities in these areas?

- **Computer skills:** Technology is a vital part of the modern world and the ability to use software, create websites, and manage social media could land you your next job. What skills would you like to gain in this area?

- **Cultural competence:** How well do you work and communicate with people who are different from you? Cultural competence involves learning about different cultures, appreciating differences amongst individuals, overcoming biases, and relating to others in respectful, affirming ways.

In addition to these general areas, certain jobs may offer opportunities to learn specific skills that could be useful in your future career. Here are examples from some of the programs described in Chapter One:

- As an AmeriCorps member serving with *College Advising Corps*, you will learn a variety of skills that would translate directly into work in the college admissions field. For example, you will learn how to advise students completing the FAFSA (Free Application for Federal Student Aid) and gain knowledge about the admissions process at colleges and universities.

- If you choose to serve with *Habitat for Humanity*, you can expect to gain construction skills, project management skills, and familiarity with different tools. These skills will come in handy whether you work in construction or just own your own home one day!

- As a member of *AmeriCorps VISTA*, you may gain experience writing grants, an invaluable skill for those who are interested in working in the nonprofit sector.

Prepare for Life after AmeriCorps

Since AmeriCorps is a short-term commitment, it is important that you use your time in AmeriCorps to begin planning for what comes next. You may begin researching potential careers, networking with those who work in your chosen career field, creating a résumé, and applying for jobs. Or, if you are planning to enroll in college or graduate school after AmeriCorps, you may begin the admissions process by filling out applications and completing the FAFSA. You will find a lot more information about preparing for life after AmeriCorps in the next chapter.

***

Now that we have explored some of the exciting opportunities that come with the AmeriCorps experience, let's consider some potential challenges that you may encounter. You may not be able to avoid these challenges altogether, but you can control your thinking about them. Remember, with a growth mindset, challenges are just new opportunities for learning.

Planning for Potential Challenges

If you have concerns about how you will manage your time, money, expectations, and relationships during your year of service, you are not alone! This section and the activities at the end of this chapter will help you to prepare for these challenges and minimize their impact.

Finances

Financial management is a struggle for many young adults, especially those who have not had experience managing money before. You may be surprised how quickly your paychecks disappear when you're responsible for your own housing, transportation, clothing, and groceries. A good way to start preparing to better manage your finances is to track the ways that you currently spend your money. Take a look at *Activity 2: Tracking your Money* on page 81 for help getting started.

Once you know what your AmeriCorps living stipend will be, you can begin thinking about how you will spend (and save) your money. The living stipend varies between programs, so it is important that you find out exactly how much your allowance is, and what other benefits are provided by your program. For example, some programs, such as AmeriCorps NCCC, provide housing, while others don't. Because the living allowance is modest, you will need to plan ahead to ensure that you can cover all your expenses and save a little for emergencies. Flat tires, illnesses, and unexpected travel happen to all of us, so it's important to be prepared.

Creating a budget will help you to plan for how you will spend your money, so that you don't come up short at the end of the month. *Activity 3: Creating a Budget* on page 82 will help you get started.

Time Management

The transition from being in school to working a full-time job can feel overwhelming at first, and you may find it difficult to juggle your AmeriCorps position with other responsibilities that you may have. Before you begin your year of service, take some time to think about your responsibilities and how you want to spend your time. What family obligations do you have? How much time do you want to spend with friends or a significant other? Do you have pets that require care? Are you participating in any clubs, organizations, or civic/religious activities? Will you be taking classes or working a part-time job while serving in AmeriCorps? *Activity 4: Time Management Preparation* on page 84 will help you plan how you will spend your time. Don't forget to leave space for rest and unexpected events that may occur.

Expectations

No matter how much you prepare for your year of service, you cannot predict exactly how it will go. You may struggle to get along with someone at your agency or you may end up doing different types of work than you expected (ever heard of "other duties as assigned"?). Maybe your office gets moved to a new location or a crisis upends your agency's priorities and plans for the year. These things happen, and it's important that you do your best to remain positive and flexible, even if things don't look exactly like you thought they would. You might also take some time before you begin your year of service to examine your expectations for the AmeriCorps experience and think about how you will respond if those expectations are not met.

Support Network

Transitioning from high school or college into the workforce can be a big transition, especially if you are moving away from the family and friends who support you. As you begin your year of service, try to be proactive about maintaining your current relationships and seeking out new ones. *Activity 5: Mapping Your Support Network* on page 86 will help you to identify people who will provide support during your year of service.

AmeriCorps Member Profiles: Their Tips for You

Now that you've read more about some of the opportunities and challenges of serving in AmeriCorps, let's hear some tips from our friends on how you can make the most of your experience.

Ariel Cochrane-Brown: College Advising Corps

Ariel's number one tip? "First and foremost, I would say: Go. For. It." For Ariel, this meant getting past uncertainty about what her role as a College Adviser should look like and whether she could handle the new responsibilities as a working adult on her own. She recommends that new AmeriCorps members keep an open mind and work to find a balance between humility and confidence. Showing humility and being willing to listen can really help you make inroads wherever you are serving. At the same time, it's important for you to "believe in yourself as much as you believe in the people you're working with."

Alex Harvey: SBP

Alex encourages AmeriCorps members to view their service as "a way to help people, but also further themselves in life." He recommends that members take advantage of opportunities to gain skills that will help with their future endeavors while also focusing on the ways that they can serve the community in the short-term. Serving with SBP presented Alex with the opportunity to try new things, live in a different community, and build a network that set him on his current career path. Keeping an eye on the big picture, and how this relatively short-term experience fits within your larger goals, can help you make the most of the year ahead while at the same time giving you the motivation to persevere through the inevitable challenges.

Andrea Rosado: Vincentian Volunteers of Cincinnati

"Where you're at in your life may feel very stressful," Andrea told us, "but trust that there is a long journey ahead of you. You don't have to have all the answers right away, and you don't have to have your dream job right away. Let this year happen to give you personal growth, professional growth, greater perspective on the world around you, and a greater understanding of how you fit into the world around you." While it can be easy to get caught up in the excitement and stress of a new job and community, Andrea stresses the importance of taking time to reflect on your experiences, and what they can tell you about yourself and your place in the world.

Matthew Hudson-Flege: AmeriCorps NCCC

Well, together with Janna, Matt has thrown an entire book full of tips at you, but here is one more. To make the most out of your time in AmeriCorps, particularly if you are coming right out of high school or college, you need to be comfortable adjusting from clear-cut, well-articulated expectations to a world of ambiguity and uncertainty. When you are a student, you have directions for your assignments, firm deadlines for completing them, and a rubric for what a "successful" assignment looks like. As an AmeriCorps member, that's often just not the reality. Yes, you will have a job description and work expectations, but defining what "success" looks like can be a lot harder when you're trying to impact a young person's life, build resilience in a community, or preserve the natural environment. Furthermore, things won't always go according to plan, no matter how much preparation you put in. Look at your time in AmeriCorps as a chance to get comfortable being uncomfortable, a skill that will serve you well throughout your life and career!

***

As you've seen so far in this chapter, making the most of your AmeriCorps experience will require both logistical and mental/emotional preparation. On the following pages you'll find several activities to help you with these preparations. In addition, here is a checklist of things you might consider before you begin your year of service:

- ☐ Finalize start date and living stipend
- ☐ Complete required onboarding paperwork and training
- ☐ Create a budget
- ☐ Find housing (if applicable)
- ☐ Make plans for moving
- ☐ Identify and build your support network
- ☐ Make a time management plan
- ☐ Set goals

Activity Reminder:

All of the activities on the following pages are also available online at www.joiningamericorps.com/activities. Use the password "AmeriCorpsActivities" to access these activities on the website.

An AmeriCorps member in City Year working with students
(Photo © City Year)

Activity 2: Tracking Your Money

Instructions: Use this chart to track your spending for a week. List every purchase you make each day and at the end of the week, add all expenses to see how much you spent. See if you can identify areas where you can save or allocate money differently.

Day	Spending (List every purchase you make each day)
Sunday	(Example: $9.50 lunch, $30 gas)
Monday	
Tuesday	
Wednesday	
Thursday	
Friday	
Saturday	
Total:	

Reflection Questions

1. *What surprised you about how you spent your money?*

2. *What (if any) changes do you need to make regarding how you spend your money? If possible, identify one specific change you will make to your spending habits. (For example, "Stop buying snacks from the vending machines.")*

JOINING AMERICORPS

Activity 3: Creating a Budget

Instructions: Use this worksheet to create a monthly budget. In the *Amount* column, enter how much you typically spend in each area, leaving items blank that don't apply. If you have an expense that you pay yearly instead of monthly (for example, renter's insurance), divide the yearly amount by 12 to determine how much you need to save each month to make the annual payment. Once you have filled in an amount for each category, calculate your total monthly income and total monthly expenses and enter those amounts in the formula at the bottom.

Monthly Expenses	Amount
Rent or Mortgage	
Renter's Insurance or Homeowner's Insurance	
Utilities (Electricity, Gas)	
Internet, Cable, Phone	
Groceries and household supplies	
Meals out	
Public transportation	
Gas for car	
Parking costs	
Car maintenance (oil changes, etc.)	
Car insurance	
Car payment	
Out of pocket health expenses*	
Medication	
Childcare	
Clothing and shoes	
Laundry	
Donations (charities, etc.)	
Gifts	
Entertainment	
Beauty care (hair, nails, etc.)	
School costs	
Credit card payment	
Savings	
Other	
TOTAL MONTHLY EXPENSES	

Note: If you are a full-time AmeriCorps member, your program provides health insurance

JOINING AMERICORPS

Monthly Income	Amount
Paychecks (salary after taxes, benefits)	
Other income (after taxes)	
TOTAL MONTHLY INCOME	

Total Monthly Income: _____

Total Monthly Expenses: - _____

= _____

Subtract your monthly expenses from your monthly income. If the number is positive, that means you have money left over! If the number is negative, you will need to make some adjustments by either finding ways to increase your income or decrease your spending.

Reflection Questions

1. *Do you have money left over or are you coming up short? If you have money left over after you have paid all of your expenses, what will you do with the surplus? If you don't have enough money to cover your expenses, what changes can you make to your budget to ensure all bills are paid?*

2. *What are your biggest budget challenges? What specific steps can you take to address them?*

3. *Are you satisfied with the amount of money you are able to save each month? Is it enough to cover emergency expenses like car repairs or illness?*

Activity 4: Time Management Preparation

As we mentioned earlier in the chapter, you may be juggling many responsibilities during your year of service. Just like you plan where your money will go, you should plan where your time will go as well! Once you know your work schedule, you can use this chart to plan how you will spend your time. Write how you will spend each hour of the day. For example, you may write "work," "exercise," "friends," "eating," or "sleep."

	Sun	Mon	Tue	Wed	Thu	Fri	Sat
6:00am							
7:00am							
8:00am							
9:00am							
10:00am							
11:00am							
12:00pm							
1:00pm							
2:00pm							
3:00pm							
4:00pm							
5:00pm							
6:00pm							
7:00pm							
8:00pm							
9:00pm							
10:00pm							
11:00pm							
12:00am							
1:00am							
2:00am							
3:00am							
4:00am							
5:00am							

Reflection Questions:

1. *Does the way you've planned your time reflect your priorities/values? Explain.*

2. *What are your biggest time wasters? How can you use your time more effectively?*

3. *Is there anything you would like to add to your schedule (exercise, involvement in organizations, a part-time job, etc.)? Is there anything you would like to remove from your schedule?*

Time Management Tips

- Use a calendar to keep up with meetings and responsibilities. Set meeting alerts and reminders on your phone to keep you from missing important events and deadlines.
- Set aside time at the beginning of the week for planning. Review all of your responsibilities for the week and develop a strategy for getting everything done.
- Make a list of everything you need to get done and then choose tasks that are most important based on their importance and urgency. Focus on the most important tasks first.
- Plan for the unexpected. Leave space in your schedule for things like traffic, illness, and relationships.
- It's important to take breaks, but avoid wasting too much time on unproductive activities like social media and TV bingeing. Allot a specific amount of time to these activities and stick to it.

Activity 5: Mapping Your Support Network

Whether you are moving to a new place or taking on a new role in a city where you have lived for a long time, it is important to find ways to nurture existing relationships, build new networks, and find ways to plug in to your local community. This graphic shows the types of relationships that might be a part of your support network. Take some time to consider what relationships you currently have as well as those you would like to add during your year of service.

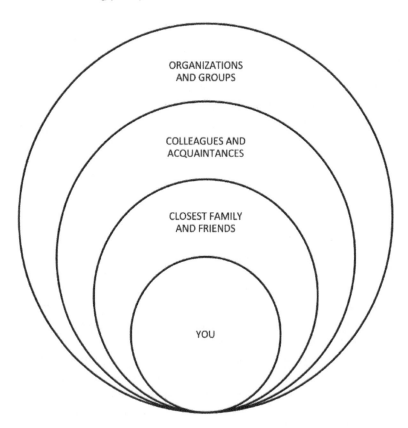

ORGANIZATIONS
AND GROUPS

COLLEAGUES AND
ACQUAINTANCES

CLOSEST FAMILY
AND FRIENDS

YOU

Reflection Questions:

1. *Who is in your "inner circle" of close friends and family members? How will you nurture those relationships?*

2. *Who did you include in the circle of work colleagues and acquaintances? What specific things can you do to build relationships at work and expand your professional network?*

3. *What organizations or groups do you currently belong to? What organizations/groups would you like to join? If you're not sure, research opportunities and/or ask colleagues or mentors for recommendations.*

Activity 6: Setting Goals

Setting goals is critical to making the most of your AmeriCorps experience. Goals will create a roadmap to guide your year of service and help keep you on track. As you are beginning your service term, take some time to think about goals that you may have in the following areas and record your thoughts below.

What skills do you want to develop?

What type of impact do you want to make?

What relationships do you want to pursue?

What steps can you take towards your future career or education?

What are your financial goals?

Once you have identified where you want to go, it's time to make your goals "SMART"—Specific, Measurable, Attainable, Realistic, and Timed. Here's what that means:

Specific: Is the goal clearly defined?
Measurable: How will you know when you've met your goal?
Actionable: Are there action steps you can take toward the goal?
Realistic: Can the goal be achieved?
Timed: When do you plan to reach the goal?

Here's an example of how you might turn a "regular" goal into a "SMART" goal:

Goal: *I want to become a better communicator.*

SMART Goal: *I want to improve my public speaking skills. During my year of service, I will seek out opportunities to practice public speaking and request feedback from my supervisor regarding voice projection, eye contact, and body language.*

List 3 SMART goals for your time in AmeriCorps here:

SMART Goal 1:

SMART Goal 2:

SMART Goal 3:

Chapter Five: Preparing for Life after AmeriCorps

AmeriCorps members serving with Habitat for Humanity
(Photo © Habitat for Humanity of Greenville County)

If you're just now thinking about joining AmeriCorps, you might wonder why we have included a chapter about preparing for life after your year of service. While we do feel that it's important to "begin with the end in mind," we also understand this might be a bit overwhelming. Feel free to set this aside and come back later as you begin your year of service. Otherwise, read on for some reflections on how to use your time in AmeriCorps to prepare for the next stage of your life and career.

What Comes Next? Discerning Career and Educational Goals during Service

If the question "What do you want to do with your life?" causes you to panic, you've come to the right place! As we discussed in Chapter Two, many young people who join AmeriCorps are unsure about what they will do after they complete their service terms. Whether you are a "Young Idealist" who joined AmeriCorps after high school, a "Wanderer" who is searching for purpose and direction, a "Gapper" who just graduated college, or a "Public Servant" pursuing a career in the nonprofit or public sector, you probably have some questions about what your life will look like after your year of service. Your family and friends may have some questions about your future plans, as well.

Choosing what to do with your life is a big decision and unfortunately, no one can tell you what career path is right for you. There are many factors that influence career decisions, and it is important that you consider how your personality, interests, values, and goals match with various careers. This section will walk you through a process of self-discovery, goal setting, and career exploration that will hopefully get you closer to making a decision about what you want to do with your life. If you already know what you're planning to do after AmeriCorps, skip to the next section (*Using Your AmeriCorps Skills in the Future* on page 102) for tips on how to leverage your experience when interviewing for jobs and applying to colleges or graduate schools.

Self-Discovery: Getting to Know Yourself

Emerging adulthood, the stage of life that happens between ages 18-29, is a time of exploration and growth for many young people. During this period, individuals may ask questions like *Who am I?*, *What do I want to do with my life?*, and *Who do I want to do it with?* Answers to these questions affect choices about education, career, and family so it is important to spend time learning about yourself and figuring out what role you want to play in the world.

Each person has a unique personality and specific interests, values, and skills that shape who they are and what type of work they may find fulfilling. Rather than trying to fit a mold of who you think you "should" be, try to figure out who you already are and look for ways to grow and develop the qualities that make you special. Do you prefer being alone or in a group? Are you spontaneous or do you like to plan in advance? Do you like to learn by reading or by doing? See below for a list of questions that will help you start the process of self-discovery! Journaling, assessments, and reflection are very helpful tools for building self-awareness.

- Do you like multitasking, or do you prefer to focus on one thing at a time?
- Do you like taking risks or do you prefer to play it safe?
- When making decisions, which do you trust more: your head or your heart?
- What feels better to you: starting projects or finishing them?
- Do you prefer to be alone or in a group?
- Do you prefer to be inside or outside?

- Are you spontaneous, or do you like to plan in advance?
- Do you learn better by reading or doing?
- Are you more of a detailed-oriented or "big picture" thinker?

In addition to learning about who you are (personality), you might also spend some time thinking about your interests (what you like), values (what is important to you), and skills (what you are good at). The following activities will help you to reflect on these areas.

Interests: What Do You Like?

This may go without saying, but try to choose a career that is interesting to you! Do you know what your interests are? They may be concrete topics like *cars, politics,* or *animals.* Or they could be more obscure concepts like *leadership* or *human motivation.* Use the space below to respond to the questions and reflect on your interests.

Values: What Is Important to You?

What do you enjoy doing in your free time? What are some topics that you feel strongly about? What past experiences have you found to be most satisfying?

Each person has values that shape their perspectives and decisions. A career that is in line with your values is more likely to be satisfying than a career that conflicts with what you believe. For example, if you value craftsmanship and quality, you may be frustrated working in a factory that mass produces poorly-made goods. If you value creativity, you may find data entry or accounting to be boring. Below you will find a list of qualities that may be important to you in a career. Check all of the ones that matter to you and then try to narrow down your checked list to three or four.

Values Checklist

☐ **Creativity:** having the opportunity to create new things (programs, materials, art, etc.)

☐ **Competition:** competing with others

☐ **Change and Variety:** having work that frequently changes

☐ **Job Stability:** engaging in work that is predictable

☐ **Security:** being assured of keeping your job

☐ **Enjoyment:** experiencing personal satisfaction in your work

☐ **Knowledge:** having opportunities to learn and deepen understanding

☐ **Aesthetics:** appreciating and/or cultivating beauty

☐ **Excitement:** experiencing a high degree of stimulation at work

☐ **Wealth:** attaining significant financial gain in your job

☐ **Working with People:** being part of a team

☐ **Independence:** working on your own with little direction

☐ **Helping Individuals:** having a positive influence on the lives of individuals or small groups

☐ **Helping Society:** work that makes the world a better place

☐ **Flexibility:** having a career that offers a flexible schedule

☐ **Decision Making:** being responsible for making decisions at your job

☐ **Physical Challenge:** engaging in physical work that uses your body

☐ **Family/Personal Life:** maintaining balance between work and personal life

☐ **Expertise:** becoming an expert in your field

☐ **Other:** _____

Skills: What Are You Good At?

Skills are the things you are good at- abilities you have that enable you to do a job. Use the space below to reflect on the skills you currently have, as well as the skills you are interested in obtaining during your year of service. Be sure to consider technical skills like computer programming or speaking a second language, as well as "soft" skills like leadership, public speaking, and problem solving. If you need help coming up with skills, check out the list of transferable skills on page 102.

My skills...

Goal Setting: Creating a Map for Your Future

Once you have gotten to know yourself, it's time to set some goals! As we discussed in Chapter Four, goals provide a roadmap to guide your decision making and keep you on track. Having a clear vision of where you want to go will help you to make career decisions that move you closer to the future you imagine. Reflect on the following questions and then use the chart in *Activity 7* on the next page to record goals in each of the five areas.

- **Finances:** How important is money to you? What kind of salary will you need to sustain the type of lifestyle you envision? What are your goals related to retirement, home ownership, family vacations, and savings? Are you financially responsible for anyone besides yourself? Do you or others in your family have significant medical expenses? If you're interested in working in public service, money probably isn't your top priority, but you do need to be able to pay the bills!

- **Relationships and Personal Life:** What types of relationships do you want to have? Will you marry and/or have children? Do you want to be near aging parents or grandparents? Do you have friends or a significant other whom you would like to live nearby? How do you envision your work-life balance? How do you see your work life meshing with other responsibilities like family, hobbies, etc.?

- **Career Environment:** What is your preferred work schedule? Do you want a traditional 8:00-5:00 job, or would you prefer something more flexible? Would you like to work in an office or some other environment? Do you want to be in a particular location?

96

- **Opportunities for advancement/promotion:** Do you want to be in a field where you can "work your way up?" or are you happy doing the same thing for your whole career? Some jobs offer more opportunities for change and growth than others.
- **Education:** How much education/training are you willing to attain? When do you hope to complete your degree(s) or certification(s)?

Activity 7: Setting Career Goals

Career Goals	In 5 Years…	In 10 Years…
Financial		
Relationships/ Personal Life		
Career Environment		
Promotion		
Education		

Career Exploration: Learning about Job Options
Now comes the fun part: matching your personality, interests, values, skills, and goals to specific careers! You can find information about different careers by talking to people in the field or using online resources like the ones listed below. Some things you might want to consider when choosing a career are projected salary, work conditions, education/training required, and job outlook. Job outlook is a prediction about whether opportunities in a particular career are expected to grow, shrink, or stay the same in the future. For example, jobs in digital media probably have a more promising job outlook than jobs in print media since people are increasingly choosing to get their news online. Take a look at the websites below to further explore careers of interest to you.

- U.S. Bureau of Labor Statistics: https://bls.gov/jobs/
- Career OneStop: https://www.careeronestop.org

Activity 8: Career Research

Instructions: Choose two careers that you are interested in and research projected salary, work conditions, education/training, and job outlook online.

	Career 1:	Career 2:
Projected average salary		
Work conditions		
Education/ Training required		
Job outlook		
Other important information		

Which of these careers is most appealing to you and why?

School or Work? Or Both?

Once you have an idea about your career path, you can decide whether you want to further your education after your service year or begin your career. You may want or need to do both depending on your financial situation, personal responsibilities, and job opportunities.

If you are thinking about going to school after you serve in AmeriCorps, keep in mind that you will be receiving a Segal AmeriCorps Education Award upon successful completion of service! This award is tied to the amount of a Federal Pell Grant, and is currently $6,345 for a full-time term of service. These funds can be used to pay back student loans that you already have, or can be used for tuition and other eligible expenses if you're planning to attend school in the future. It's important to note that the Education Award isn't just for 4-year colleges or graduate school. You can also use it at a technical college for certificate or license programs. For more information about how to use the Education Award, and what types of institutions and expenses are eligible, visit the Education Award website: https://americorps.gov/members-volunteers/segal-americorps-education-award.

Additionally, there are more than 150 schools throughout the country that are designated as "Schools of National Service" and provide some level of additional financial aid or scholarships specifically for AmeriCorps alumni. For a list of these schools, visit this website: https://americorps.gov/partner/partnerships/schools-national-service-search.

If you decide that you want to apply to colleges or graduate schools, you should start researching schools and programs at the beginning of your service year. Some schools have early application deadlines, and you don't want to miss them! Take time to research things like cost, programs available, campus activities and "vibe," and scholarships. Although the best place to find this information is on the schools' websites, there are other great resources you might use as well. At www.collegeboard.org, you can research schools and register for the SAT or ACT if standardized testing is required for admission at your preferred school. You'll also want to go ahead and complete the FAFSA (Free Application for Financial Student Aid, available at www.studentaid.gov) to make sure you access all the financial aid that is available to you. Try to visit the campuses you are interested in and talk to folks who work or attend there if possible.

If you decide to begin your career after your service year, start networking with people who are in your preferred field. Many jobs are filled through personal connections, so take time during your service year to build relationships with people who are doing the kind of work you would like to do. Finding jobs online can be difficult, so talking to people in your field is often a good way to find out about open positions when the time comes to apply.

Choosing your next step can be overwhelming. Remember, you don't have to decide what you will do forever... just find your next right step! You'll have opportunities to fine-tune your career path while in college, graduate school, or your next job.

Using Your AmeriCorps Skills in the Future

Once you've decided what path you want to take and you've identified schools and/or jobs where you want to apply, it's time to "sell" your skills and experience to employers and/or colleges. This section will help you to develop a résumé, prepare for interviews, and think about the skills you have gained during your service year that could be useful in college, graduate school, or your future career.

Transferable skills are skills that are relevant and helpful in a variety of jobs and industries. Some examples of transferable skills are problem solving, leadership, critical thinking, teamwork, communication, attention to detail, creativity, relationship building, computer skills, and management. These types of skills are useful whether you are working in a fast food restaurant, a healthcare facility, or a Fortune 500 company. Identifying and describing transferable skills is key when applying to colleges and jobs. Take a moment to review the list of skills below. What transferable skills do you possess or think you will attain during your service year?

Transferable Skills
- ☐ Time management
- ☐ Leadership/management
- ☐ Project management
- ☐ Problem solving
- ☐ Interpersonal skills
- ☐ Work ethic
- ☐ Adaptability

☐ Teamwork
☐ Perseverance
☐ Communication
☐ Event planning
☐ Fundraising
☐ Computer software
☐ Website development
☐ Social media
☐ Virtual Meetings
☐ Languages
☐ Accounting/bookkeeping
☐ Other: _____

Describing Your AmeriCorps Experience on a Résumé
Think about the transferable skills that you identified in the previous section. How will you describe them on a résumé, college/graduate school application, or in a job interview? It's not just what you say, but how you say it that will catch the attention of employers and admission committees. With a little effort, your résumé can go from basic to "wow!" Consider the impact that wording has in the descriptions on the following page.

As illustrated in these examples, it is important for you to not only explain what you did, but how what you did will be an asset in the future. For example, the description used for data entry explains that you not only know how to enter data, but you also understand social needs and have experience working on a large research project. Don't leave it up to the employer or admissions committee to decide whether your skills and experience will "transfer"; try to make those connections for them whenever you can.

Skill	Basic Description	"Wow" Description
Data entry	Entered data	Increased understanding of social needs and demographics by entering data for a large-scale research project
Interpersonal skills	Worked in a team	Facilitated meaningful communication between various stakeholders including donors, colleagues, and service recipients
Project management	Managed a project	Designed and led a long-term, multi-faceted project focused on providing afterschool tutoring to 100 local elementary school students

In addition to making sure you have a "wow" description ready for your skills, here are some other tips for creating a powerful résumé:

- Make sure you include these basic categories: Contact Information, Work Experience, and Education. Other categories may be included if relevant (Awards,

Extracurricular Activities, Leadership, Community Involvement, Skills and Certifications, etc.)

- Prioritize professionalism over creative expression (unless you are applying for a creative job!). Use a basic font like Times New Roman, Arial, Calibri, or Garamond.
- Try to keep your résumé to one page and use consistent formatting throughout. Check indents, headers, fonts, etc.
- Create a header that includes your name, phone number, and email address. You can also include social media and a personal website... just make sure they are appropriate and will help, not hurt you.
- For each school listed under "Education," include school name, degree earned (with major, if applicable), and graduation date. Don't include your GPA unless it's over 3.0.
- If you have graduated from college, you don't need to include high school information unless it is relevant to the job/graduate program to which you are applying.
- For each job listed under "Work Experience," include job title, company, location, dates employed, and a bulleted description of your job duties. This is where you will insert the detailed descriptions of your transferable skills that we discussed above. Begin each description with an action verb.
- List most recent education/work first.
- If references are requested, list them on a separate page. Make sure you include the reference's name, job title, and contact information. Always ask someone if you can list them as a reference before you do so!

- You may want to use a résumé template or create the document from scratch. Microsoft Word and Canva both offer free résumé templates.

Preparing for Job Interviews

If you are invited to interview for a position, take time to reflect on your AmeriCorps experience and think about how you will describe the work you have been doing to your interviewer. You probably won't know interview questions in advance, so you need to be prepared to integrate details about your service year into whatever questions they ask. We have included a few common interview questions below to get you started. You may want to write your answers down or practice answering the questions in a mirror (or with a friend) so you can see how you will look to an interviewer.

Practice Interview Questions:

- Why do you think this position is a good fit for you?
- How has your AmeriCorps experience prepared you for this job? Give specific examples of knowledge and skills you have gained during your service year.
- Describe your greatest strengths and give examples of how you use them.
- When have you demonstrated leadership skills? What is your leadership style?
- Where do you see yourself in 5 years? 10 years?
- What is your preferred work environment?
- What is one area where you would like to grow/improve?

- Give an example of a challenge or obstacle that you have encountered and tell how you overcame it.

Staying Civically Engaged After Service

One more important way that you can prepare for life after AmeriCorps is to think about how you will use the skills and knowledge you have gained to serve your community. As an AmeriCorps member you have committed a year (or more) of your life to public service. How will you continue to make your community a priority in the years ahead? You may find that it becomes more difficult to fit community service into your life when you are juggling work or school with family and other responsibilities. Community engagement isn't one-size-fits-all. Just like choosing a career path, choosing a path for community involvement will require both reflection and research.

When we think of community engagement, things like soup kitchens and trash cleanups often come to mind. But engagement can take many forms, depending on your community, skillset, and stage of life. As you transition from the intense experience of AmeriCorps, you may need to shift your thinking about service in order to find meaningful, sustainable ways to serve. Perhaps you will join a service organization on your campus, get involved with political advocacy efforts, or participate in a civic or religious organization. Or maybe you will volunteer at your child's school, join (or start!) a community book club, or drive your elderly neighbor to medical appointments. There are countless ways to serve. This chart will help you to consider how you might match

107

your interests/skills with needs in your community and collaborate with others to make a commitment that works for your life.

Activity 9: Matching Your Interests & Skills to Community Needs

	Example	Your Turn! (fill in an idea for yourself here)
Interests and skills: issues you care about & skills you have.	Passionate about education; love working with kids.	
Community Needs: what needs exist in your local community?	Tutoring help for elementary school kids.	
Time: how much time do you have to volunteer?	1 hour/week	
Organizations: who is doing this type of work?	Big Brothers/Big Sisters; YMCA	

There are many resources available to help you find service opportunities in your community. In addition to researching specific organizations in your local community, you may also use these online databases to find opportunities:

- United Way: www.unitedway.org
- American Red Cross: www.redcross.org
- Volunteer Match: www.volunteermatch.org

AmeriCorps Member Profiles: Where Are They Now?

We've just thrown out a lot of hypotheticals about what your life could like life after AmeriCorps. Let's check in to see what Alex, Ariel, Andrea, and Matt have been up to since serving in AmeriCorps.

Alex Harvey
After finishing his year of service with SBP, Alex was able to leverage some connections he made as an AmeriCorps member to get a job with a major property management company in New Orleans, working as a property manager. At the same time, Alex studied to get his real estate license, which had been a long-term goal for him. Alex has now settled down in New Orleans for the foreseeable future, continuing to work in property management and launching his own real estate business.

As his career settles down, and restrictions from COVID-19 begin lifting, Alex hopes to be engaged in more volunteering in the community, possibly returning to coaching little league baseball. He credits a lot of his current life to his time in AmeriCorps, having given him the opportunity to live in a new city, and giving him the experience, connections, and confidence he needed to launch his career.

Ariel Cochrane-Brown

During her time serving with College Advising Corps, Ariel began to develop a real passion for working with students. At the same time, she began to hear stories from her former students who had graduated from high school and enrolled in college, but really struggled to make the transition to college. Because of this, Ariel developed an interest in working in higher education and student success. After finishing her second year of service, she attended Clemson University for a master's in Counselor Education, and then went on to North Carolina State University to pursue her Ph.D. in Educational Research and Policy Analysis.

From there, Ariel moved to Atlanta to run a student success program at Georgia State University. After doing this work for a few years, she came full circle, and is now the Southeast Regional Director for College Advising Corps! Looking back, Ariel credits her time as an AmeriCorps member with helping her find her professional passion, and realizing how her skills and gifts could align with this passion. She now sees her current role as a culmination of her academic and professional experience, being able to both promote student success and be a support and role model for AmeriCorps members.

Andrea Rosado

While serving as an AmeriCorps member with Vincentian Volunteers of Cincinnati, Andrea was able to apply and be accepted to medical school at the University of Cincinnati, her top choice! When she got to medical school, Andrea found that she had an easier time than many of her classmates who had arrived straight from undergrad, drawing on the skills and professional development that occurred during her year of service.

Throughout medical school, Andrea was able to keep her focus on service, both finding ways to support underserved populations in Cincinnati, and also participating in international medical work in Tanzania. When choosing a specialty for residency, Andrea again was able to draw on her AmeriCorps experience, ultimately selecting a family medicine residency that fit her values of doing patient-centered and underserved care. She is now a chief resident at Christ Hospital in Cincinnati, on the hunt for a position in community and patient-centered medicine when she finishes.

Matthew Hudson-Flege
After finishing his year of service with AmeriCorps NCCC, Matt attended Eckerd College in St. Petersburg, FL. Like Andrea's experience with medical school, Matt found that he was much better prepared for life as a college student than many of his peers (or than he would have been otherwise!) after having spent the past year gaining a variety of skills and experiences. After graduating, Matt served as a Peace Corps Volunteer in Jamaica. He then returned to his hometown of Cincinnati, OH where he worked for eight years with St. Vincent de Paul, a human services organization.

Struck by a desire to better understand root causes of poverty and other social issues, Matt moved to South Carolina to pursue a Ph.D. in International Family and Community Studies at Clemson University, and now serves as Program Director of Furman

College Advising Corps. He still looks back fondly on his days in AmeriCorps NCCC, and scratches his itch for service and adventure by serving as a member of the Mountain Search and Rescue Team with the South Carolina State Guard.

***

Well, that's it! We hope that you now have all the information you need to decide whether AmeriCorps is right for you, and how to make the most out of the experience if you decide to join. As we've discussed, there are many benefits to joining AmeriCorps—from building relationships and gaining new skills, to education awards and future job opportunities. We encourage you to use this book before, during, and after your year of service to ensure that you make the most of your AmeriCorps experience. Best wishes to you as you begin this exciting journey!

AmeriCorps members serving with City Year (Photo © City Year)

Appendix One: Alternatives to AmeriCorps

Based on the title of this book, *Joining AmeriCorps*, you've probably guessed that we are pretty big fans of AmeriCorps service. However, at the end of the day, we recognize that AmeriCorps (like any program) isn't for everyone. If you've decided that AmeriCorps isn't the best next step in your life, but you're still reading this far, it's clear that even if it's not the right fit, some aspect of AmeriCorps service speaks to you. Maybe it's the chance to do national service, the opportunity to grow personally and professionally, or a desire to have new experiences. In any case, we'd like to present you with some other opportunities that are out there for you as a young adult to gain these experiences. We will start by laying out some of the most common reasons why you may have decided not to join AmeriCorps: desire to serve abroad, finances, desire to start your career, or desire to continue your education. Then, we will outline some alternative options based on each reason.

Reasons to Seek an Alternative to AmeriCorps

I want to serve abroad.
AmeriCorps is a "domestic" program, with service opportunities available only in US states and territories. If your heart is set on living and serving in another country, then AmeriCorps won't quite fit the bill (do keep in mind, however, there are opportunities to serve as an AmeriCorps member in diverse communities

throughout the States and also in territories such as Puerto Rico and Guam). If you're looking to go abroad, two national service opportunities you may consider include the Peace Corps and military service. Additionally, there are also some great faith-based international service organizations if part of your motivation to serve is spiritual or religious. We will describe each of these opportunities in a bit more detail in the next section. Finally, there are also many organizations that provide "gap year" volunteer/travel experiences that college-age young adults can pay to participate in. We won't say any more about these in this book as they may not be a realistic financial option for many of our readers, but you can visit www.gapyearassociation.org to learn more.

I can't make AmeriCorps work financially.

Perhaps the AmeriCorps positions you're most interested in are on the lower end of the living-allowance spectrum, and after doing the budgeting exercise in Chapter Four you just don't think you can make it work. Or, perhaps you have family members that you need to support or other outside financial obligations, so even with AmeriCorps benefits such as health insurance and childcare, you need to earn a higher income. In this case, a couple of AmeriCorps alternatives to consider include military service, or part-time volunteering opportunities while working in a full-time job.

I want to jump right into my career.

While we strongly believe that the professional development opportunities of serving in AmeriCorps can have a huge impact on young adults' long-term careers, maybe you're coming out of college and have been offered your "dream job." Or maybe you are interested in a career field that has very specific experience or apprenticeship requirements, such as becoming an electrician or plumber, and you want to get started right away. In either case, you can still serve your community in a meaningful way through part-time volunteering.

I want to continue my education now.

Again, we strongly believe that the skills and experiences gained during a year of service with AmeriCorps can greatly contribute to young adults' educational journey (not to mention the Education Award and résumé boost). However, we also understand that continuing your education now may make the most sense for you. This could mean going right to college or a technical training program if you're a high school senior/recent grad, continuing in school or transferring to a different major or school if you're a current college student, or beginning graduate school if you're a college senior/recent grad. As a student, you still have opportunities to serve your community while experiencing personal and professional growth. Some options include part-time volunteering, internships, and part-time AmeriCorps service.

Alternative Options

Here, we will provide a bit more information about each of the alternatives to AmeriCorps mentioned above: Peace Corps; military service; faith-based service programs; part-time volunteering; internships; and part-time AmeriCorps service. These descriptions won't be too in-depth, but we will try to point you towards some additional resources to explore further.

iii

Peace Corps

www.peacecorps.gov

Since AmeriCorps is often referred to as the "domestic Peace Corps" and draws somewhat on the tradition of the Peace Corps, it should be no surprise that this is an AmeriCorps alternative that many young adults consider. Peace Corps Volunteers serve for a little more than two years in a foreign country, with an emphasis on promoting cross-cultural understanding and local capacity building. In most cases, Peace Corps Volunteers have at least a bachelor's degree, and may be either recent college grads, mid-career professionals, or retirees. Peace Corps Volunteers receive training (language, cultural, and technical), housing (often with a host family), and a living allowance while they serve. After serving, Peace Corps Volunteers receive a readjustment allowance (money to be used to help settle back in at home), and there are many graduate school programs that have special scholarships or assistantships open to Returned Peace Corps Volunteers.

If you are debating between AmeriCorps and the Peace Corps, let us illustrate a few of the key similarities and differences for you (As a former AmeriCorps member and Peace Corps volunteer, Matt has unique insight about the similarities and differences between the programs). The main things the two programs have in common is that they are both sponsored by the U.S. government, they each provide financial support and other benefits that allow individuals to "get by" while doing full-time service, and they each have an emphasis on the personal and professional development of their members or volunteers. Key differences include the length of service (2+ years for Peace Corps) and serving domestically vs. abroad.

The other major difference, which is somewhat hard to articulate, is a different emphasis in work vs. cultural understanding. One of the original slogans for AmeriCorps was "getting things done," and AmeriCorps members are expected to make tangible contributions to the communities where they serve (i.e. the number of children tutored, houses refurbished, or miles of trail built). The Peace Corps, on the other hand, has three goals, which we will paraphrase: 1) to meet the need of host countries for trained individuals; 2) to promote a better understanding of Americans among host country individuals; and 3) to promote a better understanding of the host country among Americans. As you can see from these goals, a Peace Corps Volunteer's job is much less about "getting things done" than it is about cross-cultural understanding and training. We don't point out this distinction to argue that one approach is better than the other, but rather so you can think about which focus might be a better fit for your personality and goals. The same advice we had in Chapter Four for adjusting your expectations for what success looks like as an AmeriCorps member also holds true for Peace Corps Volunteers, although probably more so!

If you are interested in the Peace Corps, there are lots of good resources on their website to check out, and you can also find a recruiter to speak with near you.

Military Service

www.todaysmilitary.com

The oldest, most well-established, and most widespread way for a young adult to do national service is without a doubt serving in the military, whether through the Army, Navy, Marine Corps, Air Force, Coast Guard, or the newest branch, the Space Force. AmeriCorps drew heavily on the tradition of the military early in its development, particularly for programs like NCCC, and both the military and AmeriCorps have national service at their core, so it's not uncommon for young people to consider both options. Both AmeriCorps and the military provide an opportunity to serve your country, and particularly if you serve in the National Guard, your state or local community. Let's talk about the key differences.

First, there are many types of jobs in the military (fewer and fewer of which involve combat), and there are many secondary missions taken on by the military (some of which are humanitarian in nature, not unlike what you may expect from AmeriCorps or the Peace Corps). However, the primary mission of the United States military is to defend the country by fighting and winning wars. While you may or may not enlist in a combat-specific role in the military, it is important that you are comfortable with this ultimate mission, and that you also recognize there is always the chance you will be called to serve in harm's way.

Another key difference, however, is that the financial benefits of military service are generally much greater than those of AmeriCorps. While you will certainly not become rich by serving in the military, particularly as a young enlisted member, the basics such as housing, health insurance, and food will be taken care of for you (and your spouse and children if applicable) if you are serving Active Duty. Additionally, educational benefits through the GI Bill go much further in paying for a college education than the Segal AmeriCorps Education Award. These benefits typically make military service a viable option for people of different financial means.

To learn more about serving in the military, visit www.todaysmilitary.com, explore the website of a specific branch you're interested in, or talk to a recruiter in your area.

Faith-based Service Programs

If a strong part of your motivation to do a year of service comes from your faith, you may wish to explore options to do a year of service through a faith-based organization. Many different faiths offer young people opportunities to serve full-time, both internationally and in the United States, and some provide financial support and other benefits similar (although often more modest) to those of AmeriCorps or the Peace Corps. While it can be tricky to find all the options that are out there, a great place start is a list of faith-based service programs maintained by Carleton College (https://www.carleton.edu/chaplain/outreach/post-grad-service-programs/), or if you're Catholic, the Catholic Volunteer Network (https://catholicvolunteernetwork.org/). Ultimately, your best bet may be to ask a faith leader in your community or school to see if they have any recommendations. And for full transparency, many full-time, faith-based service opportunities in the United States (such as Jesuit Volunteer Corps or opportunities to serve with Jewish Family Service) are actually AmeriCorps State and National Programs, so this may not end up being an AmeriCorps "alternative" after all.

Part-time Volunteering

If you have considered a year of service with AmeriCorps, but have opted to continue your education or start a full-time job instead, there are still many ways you can serve your community as a part-time volunteer. Indeed, volunteering is a rich part of the American tradition going back to Alexis de Tocqueville's description of communities early in the history of the United States. From coaching a youth sports team to serving meals in a soup kitchen, there are countless ways to serve your community on a part-time basis through nonprofit and faith-based organizations. In addition to the impact on your local community, volunteering can also provide opportunities for your own personal and professional growth and sense of fulfillment. Just because you aren't serving full-time, doesn't mean that it can't be a meaningful experience. Indeed, for many people who do serve in AmeriCorps, continuing to volunteer is an important part of life after AmeriCorps!

To learn more about part-time volunteer opportunities, you can visit the website of your local chapter of the United Way, explore websites such as www.volunteermatch.org, or contact a local organization of interest to you. If you are a student, your school may have a service-learning office or other department that helps to facilitate volunteer opportunities. As you look for opportunities, keep in mind that while one-time volunteer events can certainly be helpful, finding an opportunity to volunteer consistently (i.e. for two hours every Wednesday evening) can allow for you to make the biggest impact through your service while also having a more meaningful experience.

Internships

If you are a college student, another opportunity to consider to both serve your community and experience personal and professional growth is through an internship with a local nonprofit organization. An internship can allow you to go a bit deeper with your work than you might as a volunteer, better understanding the issues an organization addresses and how it works, and exploring your own career interests. Additionally, there may be opportunities to earn college credit through an internship. Finally, internships can present an important opportunity to bolster your résumé and begin building your professional network.

To learn more about internship opportunities, talk to someone at your school's career center or internship office, or speak to a professor in your program. While most internships in nonprofit organizations are unpaid, there may be fellowships available (through your school or another organization) that can make an internship more doable for you.

Part-time AmeriCorps Programs

Our last AmeriCorps "alternative" is actually just another way to serve in AmeriCorps. As we mentioned in our introduction, the focus of much of this book is on full-time "year of service" opportunities through AmeriCorps that last roughly 10-12 months. However, there are many AmeriCorps programs that are part-time. These include opportunities where you serve for limited hours over a long period of time (for example, 12 hours per week for 10 months), or they may be short-term programs, typically over the summer (for example, 40 hours per week from June through August). A part-time AmeriCorps program can be a great option if you have elected to continue your education as a full-time student. As a part-time AmeriCorps member, you will receive a modest living stipend as well as a Segal AmeriCorps Education Award (which will be prorated based on the number of hours you serve). Together, these benefits can make serving in a part-time AmeriCorps position a financially viable alternative to a typical part-time job, while still offering the opportunities to serve your community and grow personally and professionally that come with AmeriCorps service. The resources in Chapter Three of this book can help you find part-time AmeriCorps opportunities in your area.

Appendix Two: A Note to Parents

By David Flege (Matt's dad)

I was wrong.

It was the fall of 2001 when our son, Matt, came to his mother and me, brimming with excitement. It seemed his big sister, Katie, then participating in the Indiana University Washington Leadership Program, had been filling his head with an idea that could only have been concocted in the DC alphabet soup of federal programs. She'd called from her cubicle at the headquarters of AmeriCorps, site of her semester-long internship, to tell him about something called the National Civilian Community Corps.

NCCC (or 'N-triple-C') if you will, is based loosely on the Civilian Conservation Corps of the New Deal era. As Matt explained enthusiastically, he would join a team of other young people 18-26 years of age, working on various projects such as the environment, disaster relief and other 'unmet needs.' Matt assured us the program would be supervised and regimented, drawing on some of the quasi-military qualities of its CCC forebear.

All well and good, except for one little problem. It wasn't college.

At seventeen going on eighteen, Matt was going through a phase, somewhere between 'Idealist' and 'Wanderer,' according to Chapter Two of this book. I certainly had my own struggles at that age, but my son... my son was smarter than me. College scholarship smart. My son was more mature than I was at that age. So, why didn't he want to get the degree and a great job? I feared he never would attend college, and I thought he was throwing away the opportunity of a lifetime. And I was wrong.

My son was also more stubborn than me, so we were sort of forced to listen as he extolled the virtues of the program. He would be joining a team in Sacramento, California (a mere 2,000 miles from home). During the year-long program, they would do various service and public works projects throughout the West. He would receive room and board, a small stipend, and—throwing a little bone to Dad—an Education Award to use for college when he completed the program.

The more he talked about AmeriCorps, the more 'Matt in college' was starting to look like 'square peg in round hole.' After coming to the realization that we couldn't force him to be successful or happy in college, we finally gave in. As if we had a choice.

So, we set aside the college brochures, packed him up, put him on the airplane, and hoped for the best. It immediately became apparent, judging by his emails and phone calls that he was thriving in the program. NCCC provided structure and discipline, and an opportunity to bond with the other young people on his team. He found the projects (mostly) challenging and worthwhile—mentoring elementary school children, trail building, reforestation, and working in a food bank, to name a few.

We had the opportunity to meet his fellow team members during a short summer visit. His team enjoyed effective leadership, and we could see that he was in a good group that got along well. Some of the friendships formed during that year have lasted to this day. At the end of the year we attended his graduation program, and, like any parents, we were proud when the team leader praised Matt for his contributions.

NCCC had been a positive experience, but with his year of service complete, we wondered what would happen next. What happened next was... he put 'AmeriCorps' on his résumé, reapplied to Eckerd College, and they increased their scholarship offer from one half to full ride! Did I mention I was wrong?

With happy hearts, we packed Matt's bags and headed south to St. Petersburg, but AmeriCorps wasn't quite in our rearview mirror yet.

Recently graduated from the School of Public and Environmental Affairs at Indiana University, our daughter announced that she was looking at various AmeriCorps programs herself. We were soon to discover that there's a city even farther from Ohio than Sacramento.

Katie served for a year with Clatsop Community Action in Astoria, Oregon as an AmeriCorps VISTA member and then tacked on another year for good measure as a NCCC support team leader in Charleston, South Carolina. Like Matt, she formed lifelong friendships and acquired professional contacts and experience that have proven valuable throughout her career.

After college, Matt applied his unused AmeriCorps Education Award to an online master's degree during his Peace Corps stint in Jamaica. Katie used hers for a Masters of Library Science. In recent years, Matt has been able to secure AmeriCorps grants that have funded programs at Clemson University and Furman University. So, twenty years later... I'm still being proven wrong.

In my defense, I didn't have *Joining AmeriCorps: A Guide for Young Adults Considering a Year of Service* to inform me. Back in the day, all we could do was trust in our children's judgment and then offer our love and support as they followed their passions. You, on the other hand, have this book. So, if your son or daughter has come to you with a brilliant idea to defer college, or defer a 'real' job after you've spent a small (or large) fortune on their education, just take your finger off the panic button and turn to Chapter One.

Like most things in life, you only get out of it what you put in. AmeriCorps is no different, and there's no guarantee that everyone's path will be successful and fulfilling. That's where this book comes in—it will be a valuable tool to help your child plan for success. It will also help you, the parent, better understand their decision. Because—let's face it—useful as a guidebook may be, your love and support will still be the most important ingredient!

Good luck to you and your family on your AmeriCorps journey.

Made in the USA
Monee, IL
14 February 2023